THE BATTLES OF NEWBURY

THE BATTLES OF NEWBURY

Crossroads of the Civil War

Christopher L. Scott

Foreword by Richard Holmes

Pen & Sword
MILITARY

First published in Great Britain in 2008 by
Pen & Sword Military
an imprint of
Pen & Sword Books Ltd
47 Church Street
Barnsley
South Yorkshire
S70 2AS

ISBN 978 1 84415 670 2

A CIP catalogue record for this book is
available from the British Library.

Typeset in Palatino by
Phoenix Typesetting, Auldgirth, Dumfriesshire

Printed and bound in England by
CPI UK

Pen & Sword Books Ltd incorporates the imprints of Pen & Sword Aviation, Pen &
Sword Maritime, Pen & Sword Military, Wharncliffe Local History,
Pen & Sword Select, Pen & Sword Military Classics and Leo Cooper.

For a complete list of Pen & Sword titles please contact
PEN & SWORD BOOKS LIMITED
47 Church Street, Barnsley, South Yorkshire, S70 2AS, England
E-mail: enquiries@pen-and-sword.co.uk
Website: www.pen-and-sword.co.uk

Contents

List of Maps

ACKNOWLEDGEMENTS

With any book there are many people to thank for help, and here I name those whom space will permit and ask those not named to forgive me.

Richard Ellis, battlefield photographer, battlefield walker and willing sounding-board for ideas and theories, for his enthusiasm and expertise in photographing the many scenes in this volume. I also thank him profusely for introducing me to Google Earth and the clues it can reveal.

Alan Turton, Curator of Basing House, long-time friend and an expert on the Earl of Essex's army, for advice and encouragement, as well as permission to freely make use of his research and the loan of many secondary and original sources.

Dr Eric Gruber von Arni, scholar and friend, for offering me unlimited access to his well-stocked military library and for teaching me the joy and skill of methodical research over the years.

Rupert Harding, of Pen & Sword, whose faith in my abilities was unshakeable and whose energy and range of interests are remarkable, and Sarah Cook, the editor, whose unseen skill has done much to improve my grammar.

Jason Clear and the Performing Arts staff of New College, Swindon, who let me 'downsize' early, never moaned when I was out on battlefields rather than rehearsing plays and let me off directing the annual pantomime.

The staff of the libraries of Newbury, Swindon Borough, and New College, Swindon, and the ever-helpful volunteer staff of Newbury Museum, who must have thought my enquiries odd but managed not to show it.

Mr Colin Clark, whom I met by chance, who regaled me with local history, tales of the battle and landscape information, and the lady in Speen who showed me her cannonball!

Mr Steve Titcombe, another chance meeting, who told me of the discoveries in the fields of Newbury II, and all those other residents whose brains I picked and whose guidance on locations I sought, including the local historian who told me about lane name changes and the postman who was a mine of information despite not knowing anything about anywhere not on his round.

Professor Richard Holmes for agreeing to find time to both read my manuscript and write the foreword.

Iain Dickie and Nigel Pell of *Miniature Wargames* for their aid with the maps, as well as the Pen & Sword production team.

And finally . . . Pamela Golding, my wife, who has listened to me talk about

Newbury, seen me disappear off to Newbury, and indeed has herself been shopping in Newbury more times than ever before, and has put up with a husband who seemed married to the PC!

This book is dedicated to Alan and Nicola Turton – it's a chantry thing.
And to his 'favourite' general . . .
the much-maligned and underrated Robert Devereux, 3rd Earl of Essex.

And you that know the gain at Newbury
Seeing the General, how undauntedly
He then encouraged you for England's right
When royal forces fled, he stood the fight!

FOREWORD

I have a particular affection for the battlefields of Newbury. I well remember visiting them – with justified trepidation, for they are not easy to interpret – when I collaborated with Brigadier Peter Young on my first book, more than half a lifetime ago. Now I drive, almost every day, up and down the A34, that traveller's friend but historian's nightmare, that crosses them. The ruins of Donnington Castle catch the summer sun and stand out against the winter snow, and however often I see the sign to Wash Common it still stirs my spirits. Perhaps this is not the place to rail against the way that we treat battlefields, and because I am delighted to escape from the great Newbury traffic jam, part of me welcomes the new line of the A34. Part of me, however, regrets the way in which, driven by ignorance cloaked in necessity, we have buried still more of our past beneath concrete and tarmac.

I commend Chris Scott's book, surprisingly the first serious modern work on these two important battles, for two reasons. Firstly because, as an experienced re-enactor, he understands Civil War armies. The soldiers of the age were neither the elegant figures depicted in contemporary drill-books, nor the tens of extras, modern folk in ancient guise, that we so often see in television documentaries – my own included. They were ground-crossing, load-bearing, horse-using creatures, who plied weapons which demanded strength and skill, and whose sense of drill and discipline often decided whether they won or lost. To understand seventeenth-century battles you must first understand seventeenth-century man, or his behaviour will at once interpose a barrier between past and present. It was still the stone age of command, with generals scarcely better served by communications than Julius Caesar had been. Maps were a rarity, and watches uncommon and poorly regulated, and most commanders relied in battle on the spoken message and shouted order. Even comparatively simple tasks, like the co-ordinated Parliamentarian attack which lay at the heart of Second Newbury, were easy to conceive but hard to execute. This is what Clausewitz was later to call friction – the fact that in war everything is simple but the most simple thing is very difficult.

Second, there is no substitute for understanding microterrain, that tiny detail embedded firmly upon any landscape, even if it is apparently featureless. A fold in the ground here or a hillock there may easily make the difference between life and death, and features like sunken lanes and hedges (particularly the thick old stock-holding hedges that laced the fields of Newbury) were really important. Sturdy pikemen defending a hedgeline were a formidable obstacle, and even the best cavalry was sharply constrained if it had no room for manoeuvre.

There are some battlefields, like Naseby or Marston Moor, where terrain has changed comparatively little, though roads and enclosures have generally altered their details. But, as Chris Scott shows us so well, Newbury was a communication hub, given its strategic importance and the routes that ran through it. These and the railway and the canal that followed later, helped encourage development which makes interpreting these battles more difficult than usual. It is in relating the ground as it then was to the landscape that we now see that the author is so successful, and he brings the battlefield to life by showing us hedged lanes and hillsides that would have been familiar to the men who fought on them more than three and a half centuries ago.

Lastly, any historian must interrogate his sources, and ask himself who is actually telling him something: how might their personal affiliation affect their judgement, and how do they know their facts? Chris Scott has based his study on primary sources, accounts written by those who knew whereof they wrote, as well as on the commentaries of fellow historians. He and I would both agree with the Duke of Wellington that it is as easy to write the history of a battle as the history of a ball, but he has, I think, come as close as we will get to the truth by applying primary sources, historical understanding and a feel for the ground to these two battles which, in their way, changed the course of our history.

As I grow older I find it harder and harder to decide which side I might have fought for in the civil war. Youthful passions would have seen me a Leveller, and by the time I reached my middle years I would probably have cheered for 'Charles, King of England, and Rupert of the Rhine!' Now I know I would wish to fight alongside my friends, for personal relationships mean far more to me than political abstractions. In that sense, I suppose, I have something in common with so many of the soldiers of both battles of Newbury, who did their duty as they saw it. When roundshot skipped across furrows and blade rasped from scabbard, men strove to seem valiant in order to gain or retain the respect of their comrades. I am sure that the bonds of mateship and the charisma of a brave leader often meant more than politics when matters came, as they so often did, 'to push of pike'. At one level I gained intellectual satisfaction from this book; at another, though, I was given a penetrating insight into the way that my ancestors would have fought across this familiar landscape. I recommend you read this book, as Chris Scott delivers two well-argued and persuasive interpretations to enable people, even the uninitiated, to understand both these enigmatic and perplexing battlefields.

Richard Holmes
Ropley, Hampshire, 2007

PREFACE

I have always been interested in battlefields. It began with pillows and books pushed under the green bedspread on my aunt's double bed, over which my toy soldiers fought many battles. Each metal warrior sought cover in what I now know is called a reverse slope, or defiantly stood on a ridge to gain the higher ground advantage in a mêlée. The 1950s films of Robert Taylor fanned the fascination and it was further fostered by the discovery of Wargaming in the early 1960s. However, it seriously took off in the early 1970s when Don Featherstone and Roger Snell started taking me on battlefield walks all over Europe. I still have the old orange and blue frame tent we used so we could sleep on the same ground 'the lads' did on the night before Crecy or Agincourt in France, Salamanca or Vittoria in Spain, Rolicia or Vimeiro in Portugal, Oudenarde or Waterloo in Belgium, and hosts of other fields. This passion has still not dimmed, for as recently as 2004 I camped on the banks of the Nebel and walked the field of Blenheim with the well-known battlefield photographer Richard Ellis, who also took the photographs for this book.

As a Trustee of the Battlefields Trust and a serving member of the Council of the Guild of Battlefield Guides, I have tried to evolve the study of battlefields into a specialist activity and indeed have endeavoured to create its own critique, based upon what I call the Three Perspectives, which embrace not only the historical evidence but also that derived from the archaeological work done on the sites and the very landscape itself. This is the Historical, Archaeological and Topographical (HAT) approach. Many battle historians have created accounts based solely upon the historical perspective, and this has resulted in several horrendous misconceptions (now steadily being amended). The leading example of this valuable revision must be the work of Michael Rayner, whose holistic study of Mortimer's Cross has resulted in a new and academically sound interpretation that rotates the accepted battle lines through 90 degrees! A pioneer of battlefield interpretation was Colonel A.E. Burne, whose books always accompanied our trips to France. He argued for something he termed Inherent Military Probability (IMP), through which he sought to get inside the military mind and apply that style of thinking to the given circumstances and the situation he saw on the ground. As IMP could offer no proof and could not be substantiated, the academic world has tended to sneer at his work, but I contend that Burne was on the right track. His fault lies not in his premise but in his application. His was a First World War artillery officer's perception of warfare and this seemed to have had a direct influence upon his interpretive skills. Immersion in the writings, memoirs, military treatises and drill manuals of contemporary generals and practitioners can help the interpreter adopt a period mind-set that allows a more focused approach to the process of trying to unravel what happened where, by shedding light on why certain things occurred and how things were done. A minor aspect of this also involves looking at the personality and track record of the general making a given decision. I call this Probable Contemporary Action (PCA), and it is steadily making me think of writing a paper entitled 'The Four Perspectives'!

Part of understanding PCA is an appreciation of the minutiae of battlefield conditions, and the problems that beset the ordinary soldier and officer in action. A writer can seldom claim to have experienced period warfare, but he could have seen an approximation to it as provided by re-enactment. Despite having made inestimable progress in terms of scale and authenticity, the world of re-enactment has received a bad press from academia, which coldly states that one learns nothing from it. I refute that on several grounds, not least by calling upon the plethora of seventeenth-century re-enactment musketeers who can speak with authority about the accuracy of their pieces, the reliability of their various locks and the penetration ability of their projectiles, as well as the varying effects of weather conditions and gunpowder quality. As somebody who has on many occasions tried to co-ordinate the movement of 650 pike- and musket-armed soldiers, I claim to appreciate the difficulties and problems involved in moving and fighting a mid-seventeenth-century regiment, even if its constituent divisions had experienced officers who knew what they were doing. I do not believe re-enactment is the great elucidator its die-hard followers claim it to be, but it certainly can give insights into PCA.

This book is essentially for people who wish to walk the battlefields of Newbury I and Newbury II. It is not intended to be a thoroughly researched academic work in the style of my book on Edgehill (Pen & Sword, 2004), which I co-wrote with Alan Turton and Dr Eric Gruber von Arni. Major controversies exist about both battles – at Newbury I, for example, did Essex's first attack go up Enborne Street as well Wheatlands Lane, and were the Red and Blue Regiments of the London Trained Bands with Essex or in the Reserve? Historians of far greater academic prowess than I have, from the same sources, produced well-constructed arguments for a number of different interpretations. One must read their arguments and make a choice. I have made my choices and I have my reasons for making them, although this is not the type of book in which to argue them. Some people will accept what I say while others will disagree, probably acrimoniously, but I have done my best to tell the story as I perceive it to be. Nevertheless, I reserve the right to change my mind should more evidence or a better-argued case arise. This is both a storybook and a guidebook, and one which I hope both embraces recent theories and research on the historical perspective of the battle and also employs proper methodology and critique for battlefield interpretation and explanation. To this end I have been joined by Richard Ellis, whose work on blending model soldiers into real landscapes has graced the pages of the wargames press, in particular the magazine *Miniature Wargames*, for many years, and whose computer skills have enabled us to add arrows and labels.

Although this book tells the essential story of each battle, I do not spend much time on describing either of the campaigns. Of course it is worth understanding why battles took place where they did, but all too often books that purport to be about battles or battlefields devote a high percentage of their pages to the events which preceded the actions, the weapons used or the soldiers who wielded them. Although I have included a section on the men and their weaponry, I prefer to focus on the action itself, and though there is never enough contemporary material for any engagement being studied, there is sufficient available in this case to gain a general idea of what happened and where. I have also, where possible, included personal stories pertinent to the fights, those moments when the deeds of individuals bring alive a distant war on a forgotten battlefield.

One of the greatest problems I encountered in unlocking the two Newburys is that several key locations have undergone a change of name, particularly in the case of Newbury I. This is further confused because contemporary accounts are written by men who fight in an area for a day and then move off, taking with them their own perception of which roads lead where and what each place or lane is called. When you realise that Biggs' Cottage stands at the southern foot of what today is called Boames Hill not Biggs' Hill, and that what some historians call Biggs' Lane was once called Bell Hill Lane and is now called Enborne Street, you might begin to understand why the battle has caused so many problems. Some secondary sources state Biggs' Hill was actually a 'Bigg Hill' and not named after anybody. Confusion also reigns over Skinners Green Lane. Locals I spoke to now use this name to refer to the winding road west of Round Hill, which runs north-south and connects Enborne Street with Enborne Road, but it was the former name of Cope Hall Lane, which runs across Round Hill and at right angles to the other road. Skinners Green used to be a much larger collection of dwellings, but as both hall and hamlet have gone, the lanes which once led to them have changed their purpose and hence their names; added to that, Darke Lane (both with and without its 'e') has vanished altogether. I have included maps to illustrate which names I use for which lanes, but the apparently movable feast that is Speenhamland on Newbury II remains a puzzle.

I also unashamedly include what Newbury itself and its environs have to offer to battlefield visitors and their families. All too often one can drive miles to walk a field only to discover there is no pub or café for lunch, no toilets and no obvious place to park a car without upsetting a farmer or obstructing a thoroughfare. I also comment upon where to stay, where to get refreshments and information, the library, the museum and what else there is to see both relating to the battle and for a good day out, although despite the admirable efforts of the tourist office staff, I concede I am not exactly flattering about battlefield-tourist services as they were in 2006/7.

I do hope you enjoy this book and with it the battlefields, but again, do bear in mind that mine is only one of several interpretations of the accounts and the ground. It is the same with most history; we have the best of intentions and strive to do the best we can. Despite that, I trust my explanations and Richard's pictures will help you share what I understand took place here, and how the ground itself influenced events. You should at least gain an understanding of the two battles and how they were played out, but more than that, you should also have the essentials for a good day out, following and retracing the marches, advances and charges of those who fought here over 350 years ago. If you want more information about battlefields or touring may I suggest you go to the websites of both the Battlefields Trust and the Guild of Battlefield Guides.

Christopher L. Scott
Swindon, 2007

Chapter One

INTRODUCTION:
THE CROSSROADS OF THE CIVIL WAR

The battles of Newbury were both fought during the First Civil War of 1642 to 1646. The first battle (Newbury I) took place on 20 September 1643 and the second battle (Newbury II) on 27 October 1644. For two battles to occur in the same place is not as strange as it might seem. Civil war armies on the move needed vast numbers of wheeled transports, including artillery, ammunition wagons and food carts, and consequently forces on campaign seldom strayed far from major roads. Newbury had an established woollen industry and was a thriving market town that owed much of its prosperity to its location at the crossroads of two of the most important arterial routes in the south of England: the major road from London to Bristol and the west, and the busy road from the port of Southampton to Oxford and the north. Throughout the region's history there has been a settlement on the site, from the time of the Ridgeway to the modern A4 and A34. Today this crossroads is even more complicated and busier, owing to the addition of Ermin Street, the old Roman road between Ilchester and Gloucester, and the now major route to the south-west via Andover and Blandford. During the civil wars Newbury also lay at the heart of a network of roads linking several strategically important centres, including Marlborough, Malmesbury, Cirencester, Abingdon, Reading, Farnham, Basing, Winchester, Andover and Salisbury, all of which were fought over and had garrisons imposed on them. Newbury lay on the road to almost everywhere and movement through the south of England usually meant going through the town at some stage.

Newbury was also the site of an important river crossing, with its bridge over the River Kennet. This river was as strategically limiting as its northern neighbour the Thames, while its tributary, the Lambourne, was bridged at nearby Donnington, where a refortified castle could house a garrison to control the region in the absence of large armies. The area was also attractive to military strategists as it was fertile and the town was more than comfortably provisioned and well off. Newbury was a rich town that could afford to feed and accommodate an army for a short while. It was thus not only an important strategic crossroads but a tempting target too.

The first battle of Newbury was the culmination of the Earl of Essex's late summer campaign in 1643. It has been called a turning point because it marked the end of what appeared to be an unstoppable run of Royalist victories:

January	Hopton beat Ruthin at Braddock Down.
March	Compton beat Brereton at Hopton Heath near Stafford, and Goring beat Fairfax at Seacroft Moor near Leeds.

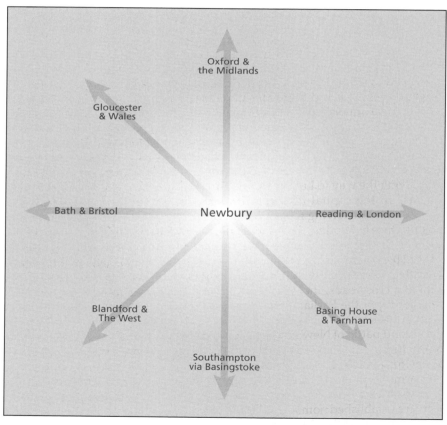

Map 1: Several strategically important roads capable of taking heavy military transport ran through Newbury and over its bridge.

April	Prince Maurice defeated Waller at Ripple Field near Tewkesbury.
May	Hopton routed Stamford's Army of the West at Stratton.
June	Rupert beat and killed Hampden at Chalgrove Field.
	Newcastle defeated the Fairfaxes at Adwalton Moor near Bradford.
July	Hopton beat Waller at Lansdown.
	Wilmot beat Waller at Roundway Down near Devizes.
	Rupert took Bristol from Fiennes.
August	Digby routed Parliamentarians at Torrington.
	Repulse of the Parliamentarian fleet under Warwick.
September	Maurice took Exeter.

In September 1643, with the West Country virtually under full Royalist control and with both Waller's and Essex's armies seemingly temporarily out of the war, the King prosecuted his siege of Gloucester. If that city fell, it would hand the King control of the River Severn and complete domination of the Marches, with easy access to and from the Royalist recruiting ground of Wales. However, Essex managed to lift the siege and prevented Gloucester falling into the King's hands, and it was while returning to London that he clashed with the royal army at Newbury for the first major battle in that part of Berkshire. Although it was a tactically inconclusive battle, Newbury I was counted a victory for Essex because the royal army marched off during the night, leaving the way to London open. Thus Essex's army was able to return to its base in the capital flushed with success, not only having relieved Gloucester but also having fought the supposedly superior cavalier army to a standstill. Once in London, the troops could over-winter in comfort and safety, and cheer the latest Parliamentarian successes: in October Fairfax and Cromwell beat Henderson at Winceby, the Hull garrison managed to drive off Newcastle's besieging forces and the Parliamentarians also took Lincoln. Fought at a crossroads, the first battle of Newbury was also a crossroads in fortune for it put the Parliamentarian cause on a firm footing for continuing the war in 1644.

The second battle of Newbury also marked a turning-point in Parliament's fortunes. In June 1644 the King successfully defeated and damaged Waller's army at Cropredy Bridge, and subsequently inflicted an even greater blow on Essex's army in the Lostwithiel campaign during August and September. In the process the Royalist forces rendered Essex's force *hors de combat* for some time and re-established nominal Royalist control of the West Country. Seeking to take advantage of this favourable situation, made even more attractive by the dispersed nature of Parliament's remaining forces in the south, the King planned a series of moves to rid the area around his base at Oxford of

Parliamentarian troops, by raising the on-going sieges of the Royalist strong-holds of Basing House, Donnington Castle and Banbury. His plans were ruined by the various Parliamentarian commanders' quick responses to a Royalist thrust at Basing in north Hampshire. In a series of quick moves they managed to get a large combined army between the King's forces and their base at Oxford, in a reversal of the situation at Newbury I. The Royalists had no option other than to fight Newbury II, a fairly conclusive encounter which, although it did not end in a rout or in the destruction of either side, saw the Royalists tactically beaten. Prince Maurice managed a strategic escape act that enabled the King and his army to return with reinforcements and force the Parliamentarians to withdraw. Newbury II was also a crossroads for the Parliamentarian army and its cause; as a result of the senior officers' poor management of the battle, the antagonism that had long been rife among them and the problems that had prevented the whole-hearted prosecution of the war were at last brought into the open and addressed by Parliament, a development that culminated in the Self-Denying Ordinance and the creation of the New Model Army.

Chapter Two

THE COMBATANTS
AND FIGHTING TECHNIQUES

Experience

The men of both sides who fought at Newbury I in 1643 were of mixed experience. Some were veterans of the Bishops' Wars, while many more had survived the campaigns and battles of Edgehill, Roundway and Lostwithiel. Many, however, were newly recruited and for some regiments, notably those of Parliament's London Brigade, this was their first time under fire. Most of the senior officers had recent military experience and understood the practical application of the 'Art of Warre'; indeed, some had already learnt hard lessons in both defeat and victory.

By Newbury II both the men in the ranks and their officers at most levels were more experienced and proficient at their job, despite Cromwell's famous remonstrance against 'old, decayed serving men and tapsters'. However, even Essex had trouble with several units in the Cornish campaign, notably Weare's Regiment, whose troops were likened to sheep. Cromwell envisaged a superior army, one that was based on professional competence and did not have to rely upon annual recruitment or still be burdened with those who held office through political and social influence. The following brief résumés seek to give the background of some of the officers, limited to what is known of their abilities at the time of the two Newburys.

The Officers

Royalists

Charles Stuart, King of England: The King began his military career as head of the army during the disastrous Bishops' Wars, during which he gained some appreciation of the problems of administration. Having little idea how to apply the theory of his military studies, he relied heavily upon those around him, seeking advice from experienced officers and court favourites. His lack of resolve proved the undoing of the royal army at Edgehill as he allowed Prince Rupert to impose the unrehearsed 'Swedish System' on its deployment, but he took more personal command during the Lostwithiel campaign, which proved successful. Despite his personal bravery, at both Newburys his direct influence appears to have been restricted to presiding at Council and making morale-boosting battlefield appearances.

Prince Rupert of the Rhine: The King's nephew was a determined man of considerable military experience. Technically, as an Anglo-German born in Prague and raised in the Palatinate, he was a foreign mercenary. He had been in the Dutch Bodyguard at 14 and fought bravely at Breda, then studied military treatises while in captivity in Vienna. He was a skilled horseman, proficient with sword and pistol, and had revolutionised English cavalry tactics by discouraging the use of firepower in attack and reintroducing the charge into combat. It had been successful at Edgehill and Roundway, and gained the royal Horse a formidable reputation. Rupert was a charismatic leader who inspired his men but he was prone to losing control and chasing off the field, taking his men with him. By Newbury II he had somewhat fallen from favour after his defeat at Marston Moor. He was stern and ambitious, no great drinker and not the romantic idol of popular fiction.

Patrick Ruthven, Earl of Forth then Brentford: A man of vast military knowledge who had seen action with the Swedish army under Gustavus Adolphus, Ruthven had held Berwick in the Second Bishops' War, was a trusted supporter of the King and, although in his 70s, was still an able soldier, if no longer at the height of his powers. Holmes styles him 'a somewhat bibulous veteran', but he had come to power at Edgehill, backing Rupert in a Council coup against Lord General Lindsey and assuming his position. Like the King, he seems to have limited his sphere of influence during Newbury I to the Headquarters. He was more active at Newbury II and did much to prepare the defensive position. He was wounded while fighting in the thick of the action.

Sir William Vavasour: Before the civil war Vavasour was a colonel in the north. At Edgehill he fought as the Lieutenant-Colonel of the King's Lifeguard, but his unit was overwhelmed and forced to flee, and he was captured. Breaking his parole, he rejoined the King and was made Governor of Hereford, and subsequently undertook an unsuccessful siege of Brampton Bryan. Earlier in October 1643 he had taken Tewkesbury with his Welsh soldiers and he and Rupert threatened to burn the houses of anyone supporting Parliament's cause. Records say he was unfit for high command, and that he was neither a good soldier nor a reliable person; the King described him as 'a man who could agree with no one in all my dominions'.

Sir John Byron: He had seen action in Dutch service and held command in both the Bishops' Wars. A former Governor of the Tower of London, he was thought – and later proved himself – to be a gallant and able soldier despite the inexperience he showed at Edgehill. He had since learnt quickly and proved himself in tactical command during Roundway and the Lostwithiel campaign. He was brave but careful with the lives of his men, which endeared him to them. Byron was one of the King's staunchest fighting men of wise council, and much the same could be said of his uncle Nicholas.

Sir Jacob Astley: An experienced soldier, Astley was at one time a teacher of matters military to Prince Rupert. Described by Holmes as 'a small taciturn man', he had served with commendable spirit and ability in the Dutch, Danish, German and English armies and was respected as an authority on training infantry. He had been Governor of Plymouth and held a colonelcy during the Bishops' Wars. He had commanded the Foot at Edgehill and had led the grand advance. He had fought bravely and manipulated the unfamiliar formation as best he could, orchestrating the retreat when the attack failed. He was determined and professional, and Newbury II proved him to be as stalwart in defence as he was in attack.

Lord George Goring: Goring had served with the English in Dutch pay and was a popular officer. Wounded at Breda, he retired to England to the post of Governor of Portsmouth and took part in both Bishops' Wars. He became embroiled in all sorts of duplicitous plots and held Portsmouth first for Parliament then for the King, eventually being forced to surrender by Waller. He fled to Holland and assisted Queen Henrietta Maria in buying arms. Returning to Britain, he was made a senior cavalry officer under Newcastle, in which role he defeated Sir Thomas Fairfax at Seacroft Moor but was captured at Wakefield. Exchanged in time for Rupert's march to York, he commanded the Left Wing at Marston Moor, where his bold leadership scattered Fairfax's troopers. Goring became the court's hero of the hour and replaced Wilmot as Lieutenant-General of the Horse during the Lostwithiel campaign. He led the King's cavalry out of the west, was instrumental in chasing Waller out of Andover and proved himself a man of action and daring.

Prince Maurice of the Palatinate: On arriving in England, Prince Rupert's younger brother was commissioned as a cavalry colonel. Wounded at Powick, he missed Edgehill, but recovered to fight at Brentford. In March 1643 he led a small independent command against Waller in the Marches, where he manoeuvred well and won Ripple Field. He then commanded the cavalry in Hertford's Army of the West, which joined with Hopton for the Roundway campaign, in which he underlined his abilities as a capable cavalry commander. His infantry commands were also successful, although his storming of Bristol under Rupert was costly to the Cornish Foot. He then took sole charge in the west, reducing several towns and cities, but he broke surrender agreements and allowed sacking to take place. He joined the King for the Lostwithiel campaign and proved once again that although he was a good soldier, he was somewhat untrustworthy and apparently indifferent to civilian suffering.

Parliamentarians

Robert Devereux, Earl of Essex: Essex was possibly the most experienced officer in the army, having seen action and had command on land and sea. He began his military career in 1620 with the Earl of Oxford in the Low Countries, where his performance as a Colonel of Foot for the Dutch was competent. Created Lieutenant-General of the Army for the 1639 war against Scotland, he was frustrated by court politics, although he was one of the few English generals to come through that war with credit. In 1642 he readily accepted Parliament's offer of command. The Edgehill campaign raised questions about his strategic prowess but any doubts were nullified by his brilliant relief of Gloucester. His success as a field commander was not in doubt and, although he had a reputation for being quarrelsome and 'difficult', he was well liked by the army and was described as 'the most popular man of the kingdom, the darling of the swordsmen'. Before Newbury II he had been seriously compromised at Lostwithiel, but although his abilities were belittled by influential politicians he was still respected by his men. He worked prodigiously to re-equip and reorganise his army, and by dogged persistence got it to Newbury, although illness prevented him from commanding there.

Philip Skippon: A thoroughly professional soldier, Skippon had spent over twenty years in military service with the Dutch, Danish and Germans. By the early 1640s he had virtually retired and taken over responsibility for training officers for the city's militia regiments. When the civil wars started he was a much-respected and experienced man. He took command of the London Trained Bands and masterminded the march to Turnham Green. After brief spells as an officer in the more 'regular' Foot and then the Horse, his potential was recognised and he became Sergeant Major-General of the Army, in which role he introduced a training programme that resulted in better efficiency and the enhanced performance of Essex's Foot.

John, Lord Robartes: At the start of the war Robartes raised a regiment for the Parliamentarian cause despite having little or no military experience. He successfully fought his regiment at Edgehill, playing a significant role in the success of Meldrum's Brigade and showing his ability not only to hold soldiers in action but to inspire them to perform beyond expectation. By Newbury II he had been installed as Governor of Plymouth, trying to keep Parliamentarian sympathies alive in the west.

Sir Philip Stapleton: Having risen quickly through the ranks of Essex's Lifeguard of Horse, Stapleton had commanded the regiment at Edgehill, where he proved he both knew and understood cavalry tactics. A good administrator and a most capable field commander, he seems to have had a good eye for ground and the ability to deploy his troops to their best advantage. He rapidly rose to Lieutenant-General of the Horse but was not a pioneer and still favoured the firepower defence; nevertheless, he had enough charisma to persuade his men to hold their fire until they could do damage and he had learnt the lessons of rallying and reforming. At Newbury II he was still an aggressive field officer who led from the front.

Sir William Waller: Waller fought with English volunteers in the Venetian army, and later joined Sir Horace Vere's expedition to the Palatinate. On the outbreak of civil war he raised a troop of horse and as a colonel took Portsmouth from Goring, but then saw his regiment scattered by Rupert at Edgehill. A good strategist, he soon became a senior officer and captured several key places in the south, becoming the hero of London and earning the nickname 'William the Conqueror'. As Major-General of the West he took Bristol and Malmesbury, scattered Herbert's Welsh at Highnam, then took Ross, Monmouth and Chepstow, but his successes came to an end when he lost to Maurice at Ripple Field. He was driven back by Hopton at Lansdown, then suffered his 'dismal defeat' at Roundway Down. He quarrelled with Essex but was appointed Commanding Officer of the Army of the Southern Association and duly defeated Hopton at Cheriton, where his insistence on proper cavalry training paid off. He was a noted tactician and a master of unexpected manoeuvres, especially night marches, although he had mismanaged his attack at Cropredy Bridge.

Edward Montagu, Earl of Manchester: As Lord Mandeville, Montagu had been a leading figure in the Popular Party in the Upper House and had fought as a colonel at Edgehill, where his regiment had run away. Position and influence not only sustained his place but won him promotion to Major-General of the Eastern Association and a seat on the Committee of Both Kingdoms. He had won at Winceby and at the costly storm of Lincoln and was Commander in Chief of the allied armies at the victory of Marston Moor. He seemed somewhat lackadaisical in operations and had doubts about continuing the war.

Sir William Balfour: A Scot who had taken English nationality in May 1642, Balfour had seen action in Dutch service and went on to become Governor of the Tower, but was dismissed by the King for 'conduct unbecoming his post' – he had refused to allow Strafford to escape! In action he proved himself personally brave, reliable and able to take the initiative and exploit developing situations. Holmes says he was 'an experienced and thoroughly able officer'.

Lawrence Crawford: A professional soldier, Crawford had been in service with Gustavus Adolphus and had fought in both the Swedish and Danish armies, as well as with the English army in Ireland. His attempted storm of York had been criticised as rash, but he was a religious man, a good administrator and an experienced if aggressive field commander.

Oliver Cromwell: A country gentleman who displayed a natural aptitude for commanding cavalry, Cromwell had fought as a captain of a troop at Edgehill and came to fame with successes at Grantham and Gainsborough and through his command of Manchester's Horse, emphasising careful selection of men and field discipline. He was still regarded as an inexperienced parvenu by his established superiors, despite having led his wing brilliantly and performed spectacularly at Marston Moor, where he had been instrumental in the victory.

The Foot

The infantry were divided into two parts, each named after its specific weapon, 'the musket' being missile-armed troops and 'the pike' being impact mêlée troops. Cooperation between the two was essential, especially in open ground. The familiar story is that the musket was the killing weapon but it took so long to reload that the musketeers were vulnerable to cavalry, so relied upon the pikemen to protect them. This is true, but the pike blocks were much more than that, as they were the men who engaged in hand-to-hand combat and killed with their long, stabbing pikes, swords, daggers or even bare hands. By the 1600s gunpowder had revolutionised warfare because even an untrained, half-starved conscript could point a musket and pull the trigger. No longer did the missile arm require powerfully built archers, while the 'noble and puissant pike', which required more practice and physical robustness to handle, was not a skilful weapon. Both the pike and the musket were the arms of the unified mass – what they lacked in quality they made up for in quantity.

The smooth bore, muzzle-loading, matchlock musket was the main weapon of the civil wars. Most were about 4 feet long and weighed about 12 pounds. Calibres, or barrel widths, varied from ½ to ¾ of an inch and were usually 12 to 14 bore (ie, the number of bullets to the pound weight). By 1643 mass production was beginning to create standardisation of each army's muskets, and this was increasingly so in 1644. The older patterns were disappearing along with their rests, and Parliament especially was able to supply cheaper styles to their soldiers. These mass-produced versions had less wood in the stocks and were consequently lighter, thinner and easier to handle. The propellant was black gunpowder, which before use was contained in lead-capped wooden bottles suspended from a leather belt worn across the shoulder, although some musketeers also used paper cartridges. Details of how the weapon was loaded and fired can be found in Scott, Turton and Gruber von Arni, *Edgehill, the Battle Reinterpreted* (Pen & Sword, 2002) but the musket of the civil war era was still a barn-door weapon that relied upon massed fire rather than individual accuracy; even 'aimed' shots were erratic. Various drill manuals extolled the matchlock musket's ability to penetrate armour at 'ten score paces' or 200 yards, but it was seldom fired in battle at more than 100. The matchlock musket may not have been as mighty as the longbow but it had advantages in the hands of common men.

The pike was regarded as the more noble weapon. Fighting with it required physical prowess, discipline and trust in one's neighbours. The pike itself was a 16-foot-long rounded ash pole, tapered at both ends and fitted with a socketed, razor-sharp steel head with protective languets and a steel butt ring or small socketed spike. Pike drill was complicated and emphasised acting in unison. It was this cohesion that made pike fighting effective. When a body of pikes engaged, the enemy saw a concentrated moving mass of sharp steel stabbing spikes pointed at them. At Edgehill the Parliamentarian pike blocks had been eight men deep but by Newbury I they had conformed to the Royalists' six. Fighting involved the men being packed together to give density and unity to a fighting block, and then pushing or stabbing the pikes forward with the weight of the men concentrated behind their points. Once again people interested in the detail of how the pike was employed should refer to *Edgehill, the Battle Reinterpreted*. Where protection was supplied, each man wore a pikeman's pot to protect his head, a gorget over his throat, a breastplate with tassets covering his thighs and groin, and perhaps a backplate. Arms were unprotected and faces were 'get-at-able', but the target of choice was the armpit, where a well-positioned thrust could drive through the ribs and into the lungs. Pikes often became unmanageable in the tightness of the press – some would bend and snap while others would get dropped – and then 'the use and execution of the pikes of the foremost ranks being past, they must presently betake themselves to the use of their swords and daggers'. The main job of the pikemen was to hold ground, and in the mêlée to break the enemy and cause disorder and exhaustion, to make them run or at least give ground. At both Newburys the pike of both sides steadfastly held their ground, usually with the help of a stout hedge behind which they were almost invincible.

By 1643 most soldiers had been issued clothing including coats, shoes, shirts and caps, but late in the year the passage of time and campaign duties would doubtless have taken their toll on the men's appearance. The ordinary soldier's coat of the period was straight fitting and skimpily cut from heavily felted wool cloth with prominent shoulder rolls. In most cases it was lined with a contrasting coloured cloth, but both coat and lining colours varied as the supply of cloth was erratic and it would not be unusual to see regiments comprised of companies wearing coats of different colours or, like Springates', to be dressed in white one year and red the next. Most of Essex's men at Newbury I wore grey or red coats lined with red or yellow, owing to a clothing issue at Bierton in late August, while at the Portsmouth reclothing they were given mostly grey coats in time for Newbury II. In 1643 the royal Oxford Army had been issued with 'suits' of matching coats, breeches and caps, 2,500 in red and 1,500 in blue, yet one source states that four regiments wore white (ie, undyed wool). The following table of coat colours for the Newbury I regiments is derived from the findings of Alan Turton and John Barrett, working independently on the analysis of accounts, orders and issue documents and witness statements.

Newbury I

Parliamentarian Horse	
Essex's Lifeguard	Red?
Meldrum's	Blue?
Goodwin's	Green?

Parliamentarian Foot	
Langham's	Blue lined white
Barclay's	Red lined blue
Holmstead's	Red lined white
Essex's	Orange
Tyrell's	Green lined yellow
Brooke's	Purple
Skippon's	Red lined yellow
Springate's	White
Constable's	Blue
Robartes'	Red lined yellow
Martin's	Grey lined white
Mainwaring's	Red lined white

Royalist Horse	
King's Lifeguard	Red
Rupert's Lifeguard	Black
Rupert's	Blue
Queen's	Red
Caernarvon's	Green?
Maurice's	Red
Prince of Wales's	Red
Northampton's	Green?
A. Aston's	Blue?
Hopton's	Blue
John Byron's	Blue
Vaughan's	Blue
C. Gerard's	Blue

Royalist Foot	
King's Lifeguard	Red
Forth's	Red?
Jacob Astley's	Blue?
Vavasour's	Yellow
Prince of Wales's	Red or Blue?
Lord Percy's	White
Blackwell's	Black
C. Gerard's	Red or Blue?
Grandison's	Red?
Bolles's	White or Grey?
Lunsford's	Blue
Dutton's	White
Owen's	Green?
Dyves'	Yellow?
Blagge's	Yellow
Molyneux's	Blue?
Tyldesley's	Red?
Darcy's	Blue
Pinchbeck's	**Grey**

Beneath the coat the soldier would have worn a woollen or linen waistcoat, if he possessed one, over the linen or hemp issued shirt. Some breeches were issued to the Foot, especially by Newbury II. Stockings, often promised but not always received, were either knitted or cut on the cross from linen or flannel, and held up with a garter sash. Infantry shoes were usually of the low-fitting latchet variety, straight-lasted and made of leather. Headwear was also varied and included broad-brimmed felt hats, various styles of knitted Monmouth caps and Montero caps which were popular with the military. Armour in the form of helmets, back- and breastplates was supplied to the pikemen on both sides when available, although on the King's side there was a definite shortage. Musketeers wore little or no armour and carried their powder in bottles dangling from a collar or shoulder belt, called a bandolier and worn over the left shoulder, or as cartridges in a leather bag or box. Leather buffcoats were popular with officers (who often had their own coat sleeves laced into the bodice), but the only infantry rank and file known to have worn buffcoats were the richer members of the London Trained Bands who fought at both Newburys.

The Horse

Earlier in the seventeenth century Gustavus Adolphus's Swedish cavalry had shown how the Horse could be a battle-winning shock-action weapon. Eschewing the firefight dogma of the period drill manuals, they trotted forward to fire pistols at close range and then spurred into the enemy, over-coming them with impetus and the sword. Prince Rupert of the Rhine imported this practice into England at the start of the civil wars, but added the refinement of increasing the speed of the charge and saving the pistol for the mêlée.

The battle of Edgehill in 1642 had sounded the death knell of firepower cavalry, but Parliament's Horse had been issued with pistols and carbines and were consequently loath to abandon the traditional fighting technique. Indeed, they used it effectively at Aldbourne Chase. The majority of the cavalrymen had been recruited from farming or merchant communities and brought their everyday horses to the wars. These were not the thoroughbreds of the aristocracy and tended to be somewhat smaller, less powerful and quieter. However, the troopers were well equipped thanks to Parliament's control of London and its manufacturing industries. Back- and breastplates were drawn from the Tower and other centralised armouries, and although many men wore broad-brimmed hats on campaign, for battle these were exchanged for cavalry pots, with articulated neck-guards and English tri-bar face-guards. Most cavalrymen wore their own clothes but they might have attained a vaguely uniform appearance through the practice of wearing red breeches (which became popular in the Bishops' Wars) and the ready avail-ability of grey coats and cloaks, some without sleeves.

A substantial portion of the Royalist cavalry came from the wealthy landed gentry and their retainers. They rode their own horses, wore their own clothes and sported whatever armour they could find from their families' or neigh-bours' past military service. Other than the King's Lifeguard, they had no central purchasing and no supply depot, and there are no known records of clothing issues. In reality the royal cavalry were a far cry from the jaunty cavaliers depicted by Victorian artists, and the Gloucester and Lostwithiel campaigns must have taken their toll on their appearance as well. Most wore breastplates and many the tri-bar helmet, although the European single-nasal helmet would also have been in use. Few carried firearms, although the odd pistol might be tucked into a boot, and their principal weapon was either a short mortuary sword or the more expensive Pappenheimer rapier. By Newbury II the poleaxe (or pollaxe), a short battleaxe, was dropping out of favour.

On the battlefield many of the Horse of both sides wore the one desirable universal item of troopers' apparel, the sleeved, long skirted, leather buffcoat.

Made initially of water-buffalo (later ox) hide, it was layered sufficiently to provide good protection against sword cuts. It was often dyed and ranged in colour from buff to bright yellow, and it was frequently waterproofed, sometimes with grease. Parliament established fairly regular supplies of cavalry buffcoats, although Royalist troopers apparently had to purchase their own. Buffcoats were a growing trend at Newbury I and by Newbury II most troopers had them. Distinguishing the two sides thus became difficult, so the cavalry adopted the fashion of wearing brightly coloured waist scarves, usually of taffeta. Their colour proclaimed their allegiance: many of Parliament's cavalry wore orange-tawny scarves, while a lot of Royalists wore red.

We are not told how the cavalry forces were tactically deployed for the battles of Newbury but as both involved fighting along lanes, among hedgerows and in small fields it might be that the Parliamentarians were six ranks deep, so that by firing by ranks and then retiring to allow the next rank to shoot they could lay down a substantial amount of fire. The ground probably also dictated that their frontages were narrow, each troop being approximately nine files wide, thereby enabling them to ride three abreast through lanes and gateways. In the centre Byron may have adopted the same formation but Rupert is known to have favoured the thinner, three-deep deployment, and on his more open ground his troops would have formed as many files as possible from the number of men available.

Royalist cavalry attacks on both battlefields seem to have followed the same pattern. They began at the walk, then a slow trot preceded a 'good round trot', until individuals or pockets of men spurred into the canter or even the gallop. At Newbury I Stapleton had his men keep their mounts stationary for the firepower defence, which not only incorporated their own pistols but was supported by musketry from the nearby Foot and Dragoons. Fire had to be delivered at such a range that the majority of balls would not only hit a target but also penetrate it. At Edgehill the Parliamentarian Horse fired too soon but at Newbury I their shooting was effective. Despite being driven off several times, the Royalists' determination and élan finally meant they got in among their foes, aided by another feature of what has been called the English cavalry system. By refusing firepower support, the speed of the charge is increased and thus the time it takes to come into contact is reduced. There are no delays to rein in to deliver a pistol volley or to wait for footsoldiers to keep up or to fire. By Newbury II both sides seem to have abandoned firepower as their principal tactic and rapidly closed with cold steel and pistols to hazard all in the fury of a mêlée. It would appear, however, that the Royalist troopers still had the advantage in horsemanship and horseflesh.

Some writers have criticised Maurice and Goring for not launching more attacks in the early evening of Newbury II when the Parliamentarian horse had fallen back. I disagree. Contemporary military manuals state that an army whose Horse had run would lose its communications, supply lines and war chest, and would surrender. But Cromwell's and Balfour's men had not run, and, like Stapleton's at Newbury I, they had reformed and were capable of returning. If the Royalists had gone forward, they might have met with a devastating reverse and incurred losses their army would find hard to replace; even a victory might have escalated into a chase which might have seen Waller's horse off but would also have deprived the royal army of its own cavalry – a state of affairs it could not afford.

Dragoons were mounted but were not considered part of the Horse. Their use was still in its infancy but they served as 'mounted infantry'; their technique was to ride to their appointed position, dismount, tether their horses and then fight on foot, often in loose order groups making what use they could of cover and terrain features. If threatened, they were to retire, remount and withdraw. The enclosed ground of both Newburys suited their battlefield role of securing the flanks of armies and breaking up attacks by enfilading an enemy advance from cover. The Parliamentarian dragoons performed exceptionally well at Newbury I: using an early version of fire and movement they took and secured essential lanes and covered or shut down gaps in hedges. We do not have much information about their role on either side at Newbury II.

Despite the growing use of dragoons, the success of the unsupported shock-action mounted arm did not result in a total abandonment of cavalry firearms but it did help implant the belief that the charge could overcome firepower, if only it was done with spirit and determination.

The Artillery

Artillery design and manufacture had not advanced greatly since the time of Henry VIII but the development of the poundage system and some agreement on calibres and weight of shot in respect to charge had been made. Two distinct types of gun were emerging: those to fire against troops and those required to batter walls or lob bombs into works, but they had not yet developed the exploding shell. A further distinction between field guns was also developing: there were heavy guns for long range and battery work and light guns for close infantry support. Accuracy depended not only upon aim but also on the precision-casting of the barrel, the quality of powder and the calibre of shot. The details given in the table opposite are taken from Ward's *Animadversions of Warre*, edited to give a simple picture of what was available to the gunners at both Newburys.

There was no standard arrangement for manning a gun. From various accounts we can arrive at the approximation that a big gun, such as a demi-culverin (10 to 12pdr) had about eight men serving the piece: five working the gun directly and three carrying ammunition. The period authority, W. Eldred, states, 'one may well make 10 shots an hour if the peeces be well fortified and strong, but if they be ordinary peeces then 8 is enough, always provided that after 40 shots you refresh and cool the peece and let her reste an houre'.

The casualty effect of round shot was not as devastating as the bursting shells of later periods. A ball might hit one or two men, although in extreme circumstances a single ball passing through a formation could kill or maim a complete file of six, with the shock wave also knocking over the files on either side. These men would later get up, and were not even classed as 'wounded', but they would have been effectively removed from the fight for some time. However, the ability to inflict casualties was small compared to the effect guns had on morale. The noise and the smoke produced must have terrified men and horses. When this is added to their ability to hit from such a long distance, the fear induced by the very presence of guns must have been substantial, let alone the psychological demands placed on men such as those of the Red and Blue Regiments of the London Trained Bands at Newbury I who were ordered to stand firm in the face of the guns and take it.

Type	Bore (in)	Shot Weight (lbs)	(lbs*)	Charge Range (yd)	Point Blank	Utmost Range (yd)	
Demi-cannon	6		27	18		340	1,700
Culverin	5		15	12		400	2,500
Demi-culverin	4½		11¾	9		380	1,800
Saker	3¾		5½	5½		300	1,500
Minion	3¼		3	5		280	1,400
Fawcon	2¼		2½	2½		260	1,200
Robinet	1½		¾	¾		150	700

* In lbs of Serpentine (not corned) powder.
Source: National Archives, S.P. 12/242, ff. 64–5; R. Ward, *Animadversions of Warre* (London, 1639); W. Eldred, *The Gunners' Glasse* (London, 1646); A.R. Hall, *Ballistics of the Seventeenth Century* (Cambridge University Press, 1952).

The 'Traynes' of both sides took responsibility for the provision of ammunition to the whole army. The task of transporting ammunition and the heavy guns about the countryside was a mammoth one requiring exceptional organisational and administration skills and a more than basic understanding of engineering, animal husbandry and diplomacy. It also needed vast quantities of material, and seemingly limitless numbers of horses, carriages, wagons, drivers, carters, pioneers, craftsmen and labourers. It was a very expensive arm which Clarendon calls *'a spunge that could never be . . . satisfied'*. At Newbury I the Royalists had outrun their supply capabilities and consequently when they grew short of ammunition, and particularly gunpowder, they could not get sufficient supplies to the battlefield despite Herculean efforts at the Oxford depot.

Colours

The flags carried by both sides followed the normal English style of the seventeenth century. Infantry colours were about 6 foot 6 inches by 6 foot, made of silk and mounted on a short pike. In every battalion each infantry company had its own distinctive flag with a junior officer, called an ensign, to carry it. Although most colours had the St George's Cross stitched in the top canton next to the staff, the colonel's company often flew a plain single tincture 'colour'. The lieutenant-colonel frequently had only 'a George in canton', while a major usually had a 'pile wavy' emanating from it. Across the regiment the remaining company flags differed slightly in a systematic way, using increasing numbers of motifs displayed in their fields to signify the 'dignity' of the commanding captain – first captain, second captain, third captain, etc. These motifs were often simple shapes, like roundels, stars or lozenges, although devices drawn from the colonel's coat of arms or crest were known. Regiments were sometimes known by the tincture of their flags, for example the Blue Regiment or the Red Regiment.

The flags (or cornets) carried by the cavalry differed greatly from those of the Foot. There was seldom a regimental flag as each constituent unit was usually raised by an individual and their allegiance was primarily to the troop. The cornet of each troop was about 1 foot, 6 inches square, made of silk and usually edged with a heavy parti-coloured fringe. Each captain would have his cornet skilfully painted with his own *'impresse'*, sometimes an armorial achievement, a romantic or heroic motto or a political cartoon. The cornet was attached to a medieval-style lance by silk cords and tassels. Dragoons' colours or guidons were similar in size to the cavalry cornets but were more elongated, generally with two swallow tails, and with their devices resembling those of the infantry.

All these flags were essentially recognition symbols and rallying points but they were also highly prized and looked upon as trophies to be guarded or captured with great heroism. It is doubtful that they had yet taken on the almost mystical quality of regimental spirit and soul as imparted to them by later generations, but their capture was highly rewarded. Those seeking to learn more about the appearance of civil war military flags, and their construction, use and association, are recommended to see the work of Dr Lesley Prince of Birmingham University.

Field Signs and Words

Because this was a civil war the two armies frequently could not be told apart. Most of the participants were English so their weapons and clothing, whether issued or not, were very similar. Consequently each army adopted some distinguishing item to wear about their person. Officers' and troopers' scarves were often colour-coded: tawny-orange denoting allegiance to the Earl of Essex became a popular Parliamentarian colour, while red, pink and blue were popular among the Royalists. However, some general officers also had their followers wearing coloured scarves. Cromwell's, for example, are known to have worn silver, and Fairfax's blue, while red was a universally popular 'English' colour. Fighting men need to be able to identify the enemy. At night one side could simply pull out their shirt tails to prevent 'blue on blue' attacks, but the more usual practice was to jam a piece of paper or greenery in their headgear and shout a recognisable party slogan, such as 'God and Parliament' or 'The King and the Cause'. The evidence is not definite, but the following are believed to have been used at the Newburys.

Royalist:	Field Sign	Field Word
Newbury I	Unknown	'Queen Mary!'
Newbury II	Astley's Command: shirt tail out?	Unknown

Parliamentarian:	Field Sign	Field Word
Newbury I	Sprig of furze or broom	'Religion!'
Newbury II	Unknown	Unknown

Sometimes even these can become confused. For example, Money maintains that at Newbury I both sides used the same field words as they had supposedly used at Marston Moor – 'God with Us' for the Parliamentarians and 'God and the King' for the Royalists. This seems unlikely but it is possible – if only Money had quoted his source.

Chapter Three

HOW DO WE KNOW?

In general terms, the earlier the battle the more difficult it is to gather good first-hand contemporary descriptions, known as primary sources. Most military historians have heard the Duke of Wellington's famous comparison between writing a history of a battle and that of a ball. The number and variety of experiences plus the level of confusion among the participants is just too great and too localised for them to give a clear overall account, while personal interest colours most comments with intentional or unintentional bias. However, although not as numerous as we would like, the sources for the two Newburys are reasonably good and tend to substantiate one another, even if they come from opposing sides. The seventeenth-century historian Thomas May wrote that the Royalists confessed enemy sources 'to be full not only of modesty but truth in general, or for the most part'. Although these are by no means the only ones, the major primary sources that are easily accessible for more general readers are as follows.

Newbury I
Royalist:
Lord Digby (attributed), *A True and Impartial Relation of the Battaile betwixt His Majestie's Army and that of the Rebels neare Newbury in Berkshire,* taken from 'A Letter from the Army to a Noble Friend' (Oxford, 1643).
Sir John Byron, *An Account of the battles of Newbury,* written about 1647 for Clarendon when compiling his history.
An account from another letter written by an unknown Royalist officer.
Parliamentarian:
The Parliamentarian Colonels, *A True Relation of the Late Expedition of His Excellency, Roberte Earl of Essex, for the Relief of Gloucester* (London, 1643).
Henry Foster, *A True and Exact Relation of the Marchings of the Two Regiments of the Trained Bands of the City of London* (London, 1643), in J. Washbourne, *Bibliotheca Gloucestrensis* (London, 1823).

Newbury II
Royalist:
Sir Edward Walker, *Historical Discourses upon Severall Occasions* (1705).
Richard Symonds, *Diary of the Marches of the Royal Army* (1644).
John Gwyn, *The Military Memoirs of Captain John Gwyn* (1660s).
Parliamentarian:
Simeon Ashe, campaign chaplain to Manchester, *A True Relation of the Most Chiefe Occurences, as at and since the late Battell at Newbery Late.*
A Letter sent to . . . the Speaker . . . wherein is truely related the Great Victory . . . by the Parliaments Army against the Kings Forces, neer Newbery, which was read to the House (London, 1644).
Philip Skippon, *Letter to the Committee of Both Kingdoms, Oct. 30th 1644.*
Sir William Waller, *Recollections . . .*
The *Memoirs of Edmund Ludlow,* ed. C. Firth (Oxford, 1894).

    Added to these works we have more contemporary sources in the daybooks of participants, such as Prince Rupert's Diary, and in the weekly newsbooks of both causes, such as the *Mercurius Aulicus* (a somewhat 'spun' Royalist account of Newbury I, although a good report on Newbury II) and the *Mercurius Britannicus*, as well as propaganda pamphlets, gossip sheets, published letters and the information collected and published by period historians, notably Edward Hyde, Earl of Clarendon, *The History of the Rebellion and Civil Wars in England* (Oxford, 1888), Vicar, *Parliamentary Chronicles* (London, 1644) and Whitlock, *Memorials of the English Affairs* (1682). There are also contemporary biographies, such as Walsingham's life of Digby, *Hector Britannicus* (1645), but often these are rather too concerned to laud or vindicate their subject's conduct. The Calendar of State Papers Domestic is useful for examining official affairs of state and is fascinating on Cromwell's charges against Manchester after Newbury II. Readers should be wary of bias and partisanship in all sources, although overall 'official' accounts are adjudged to be reasonably accurate. That both sides read what the other had published is obvious. The opening of the Parliamentarian official account says it wishes to correct already published misperceptions, and the four commissioners' *Letter to the Speaker*, written one day after Newbury II, claims Goring's brother was shot dead during a charge, while *Mercurius Aulicus*, written a couple of days later, says he is alive and will prove it with another charge!
    Among the many secondary sources we have the works of such respected historians as John Barratt, Keith Roberts, Ian Roy and Alan Turton, whose published findings and argued thoughts have illuminated several battles of the English Civil Wars. Nor must we forget the Victorians, among whom Walter Money stands out; his *First and Second Battles of Newbury* (London,

1881), despite its penchant for romance, is a fount of local topographical knowledge and local oral tradition, and adds a lot of colour. It is evidence-based but it cannot always be treated as reliable; like most historians he makes mistakes and new things have come to light since he studied and wrote.

Studying battles calls for accurate contemporary maps but the further back in time we go the more difficult it is to find period cartographers at work. The most easily accessible interpretation, published by Osprey to illustrate Roberts' *First Battle of Newbury 1643* (2003), looks strangely modern with angular hedge patterns, roads similar to those which exist today and period lanes which follow modern footpaths. Although nicely executed, with well-defined slopes and distinctive roads, the undated map by E. Waller is much earlier but it is also somewhat misleading as it seems to depend upon post-Enclosure hedges and country lanes. Possibly more useful is the Whiteman and Bass map of 1877, which does attempt to show contours for the central battle area. However, it is covered with regimental and troop markers which, despite being speculative, give the impression of being based upon solid evidence. If this evidence exists on contemporary maps or documents it would be wonderful if somebody could discover where it is.

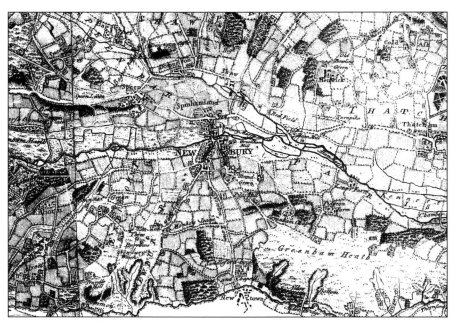

Map 2: The Rocque Map of the general area.

Unfortunately seventeenth-century mapmakers seldom went into the sort of detail we need for battlefield study and the only one for 1644 shows the principal rivers of the region and pinpoints only Newbury itself and the surrounding major villages. The town museum has the John Ogilby one inch to a mile strip map of 1675 but it is not very informative, and also displays a large scale, coloured, detailed field map drawn for the Chandos family of their manors and holdings around Newbury in 1730. The earliest useful map of the whole area I found was the Rocque Map published in 1752/3 and in 1761, which purports to show most major and minor roads, steep slopes and marshes, rivers and streams, copses and commons, as well as plantations and field boundaries. Indeed, if it could be proved to be as accurate as it is detailed, then it is a marvellous piece of work. It is particularly useful in understanding the route of Waller's night march, for it apparently went by the main roads of the day in order to move its accompanying cannon more easily. It is certainly the most useful map for our purposes and I have made much use of it.

John Willis's 1768 map of Newbury is useful for indicating the possible location of buildings but it was drawn more than a hundred years after the battles. I have been told that another more pertinent map exists but it is currently a closely guarded academic secret. I look forward to its publication.

Another source of information and a very useful tool for helping to understand battlefields is satellite photography, which can give extraordinary detail and help trace field works and long-eradicated tracks and roadways. Both Microsoft Local Live and Google Earth have good definition on Newbury and they can help determine just how much ground various formations covered by superimposing scaled-size regimental or brigade blocks. This tells us, for example, that in order to meet the demands of some of the early maps of the battle, Essex's regiments would have to have stood just two deep to have filled the shown occupied ground. Another useful aspect of Google Earth is the ability to 'tilt' the image and then advance up lanes, over rises and dips, following the route of various commanders to the places where they fought.

Of course, we can never actually know what happened, and although there are quite a few sources of information, both contemporary and modern, the best we can do is take what we are offered, apply what we understand about the period and then walk the ground time and time again trying to bring it all together so as to make sense of everything – always appreciating that someday artefacts or documents may be discovered which throw everything up in the air. Thus I do not publish in order to say I have got it right, or to join any academic fraternity, but rather to share my enjoyment of battlefield walking and perhaps help others come to their own appreciation and understanding of what went on.

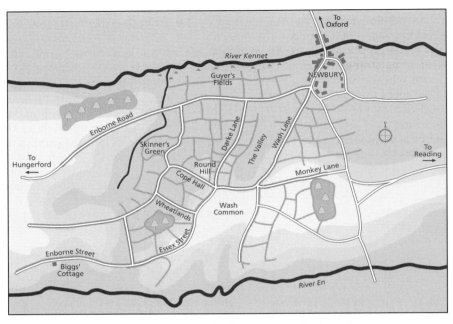

Map 3: The names used in the text for the lanes across Newbury I.

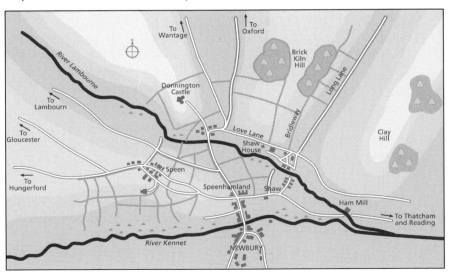

Map 4: The names used in the text for the lanes across Newbury II.

As mentioned in the Preface, the names of the various lanes have changed over the years for a variety of reasons. Most historians, of course, tend to use the names applicable in their period and this has resulted in much confusion and some strange troop placing and movements, a process exacerbated by those whose research has been limited largely to written sources and who have spent minimal time walking the fields, gauging or pacing out unit sizes and deployment distances. A part of this essential practice has involved working off a set collection of lane names which, although they might challenge several writers' perceptions, are at least constant. These are published on page 24.

Chapter Four

THE FIRST BATTLE OF NEWBURY

The Campaign

Spring 1643 had seen Robert Devereux, Earl of Essex, and his 'marching army' victorious in the taking of Reading and its royal magazine (27 April 1643), although he did allow the defeated garrison to march out to join the King at Oxford. However, sickness, believed to be typhus, then ravaged his army and prevented any follow-up strategic moves or indeed attempts to aid Waller against Hopton. It could be argued that this bout of camp fever, coupled with some sound campaign moves by King Charles I and his German nephew Prince Rupert of the Rhine, led to the pinnacle of Royalist success during the war. A Royalist council of war decided to capitalise on their successes by mopping up all centres of resistance before launching a major attack on London. Rupert's brother Maurice was given command of the Army of the West and dispatched to Dorchester to eradicate all Parliamentarian garrisons in Dorset, while the King and the Army of Oxford concentrated on taking the city of Gloucester, which dominated the Severn Valley. However, by August 1643 Essex's men had recovered sufficiently to begin further operations and they were able to undertake a march to relieve the city of Gloucester, which stood alone as a beleaguered bastion of Parliamentarian control and influence in the west.

Reinforced by a considerable contingent of the London Militia, both Trained Bands and Auxiliaries, Essex's army set out from a general rendezvous at Brackley Heath near Aynho on Friday 1 September. They reached Chipping Norton on the 3rd, and by the 5th they were at Prestbury. Here they fired four big guns to let the Royalists know they were there, and even drew up in battle formation on a hillside so the enemy could see them, before continuing their march towards their goal. As it could not both maintain the siege and defeat the relieving force, the King's army abandoned the city. Essex and his men marched in to a fêted triumph, and the good citizens of Gloucester were able to inscribe on their South Gate the immortal words, 'A City assaulted by Man, but saved by God!' They also incised there the plea 'Ever remember the Vth Sept. 1643' – a pledge honoured by a public local holiday until very recently. Essex's relief of Gloucester was a major achievement. His army had marched in appalling weather from London to the Severn and caused the King's forces to withdraw before them. Once inside the city walls Parliament's precious army was safe from attack. However, the Royalists knew Essex had to come out again, most probably with the intention of returning to London. The King and his advisers realised that if they could destroy his forces, Parliament's major field army, in open battle, the entire war could be brought to a speedy and dramatic end. They also knew that, just as they had done at Edgehill in October 1642, they only had to place themselves between Essex and London, severing his lines of communication and cutting off his line of retreat, and Essex would have to fight. The main problem for the Parliamentarians was the King's central power base at Oxford, which was by 1643 ringed by garrisons. This meant that any west–east marches by Parliamentarian troops had to loop either north or south of that malignant bastion.

However, Essex was a wily character. On 10 September he marched out of Gloucester, heading north for Tewkesbury, where he threw a bridge of boats over the River Severn, hoping to mislead the Royalists into thinking that he intended to move next to Hereford and threaten one of the King's most fruitful recruiting regions. The Royalists, then grouped around the small Cotswold market town of Sudeley, were not fooled and the King ordered a move to Pershore to thwart any attempt by Essex to take the Evesham and Warwick route home. Parliament's Lord General had, however, pre-selected the southern loop around Oxford and the army promptly left Tewkesbury heading south-east. Catching the King's army on the wrong-foot, they reached Cirencester on the night of the 15th. Early the next morning, under the command of Sir Robert Pye, they rushed the sentries and carried the town. There were few casualties on either side but Pye was wounded in the arm. The surprised Royalist garrison was still a-bed, and the Parliamentarians secured some 200 prisoners and stocks of supplies, including twenty-seven wagonloads of foodstuffs and other provisions that had been stacked in the schoolhouse. Essex quickly pressed on, despite the rain, crossing the Thames at Cricklade and reaching Swindon on 17 September. The King's army reacted surprisingly quickly and chased them on an approximately parallel course; the Royalists spent the 17th at Alvescot. On that cold and frosty night the main armies slept about 10 miles apart.

Both sides were racing for Newbury and the Great West Road to London (now the A4), and it looked as if Essex was going to win; he had only about 20 miles to cover while the King had nearer 30 via Faringdon and Wantage. In order to slow Essex's progress across the north Wiltshire downs the King dispatched his nephew Prince Rupert with what today we would call a 'flying column', consisting mostly of Horse, to intercept and harass them. Rupert moved quickly, crossing the Thames at Faringdon. Hearing that Essex's men were in Swindon, he sent out patrols after them and then cut across country to intercept them between Chiseldon and Aldbourne, just south of the now-levelled village of Snap. Rupert's van under Urrey surprised the Parliamentarian column on the 18th as it moved through the valley of Aldbourne Chase; not expecting to see the enemy, Essex's men had no scouts out beyond their rearguard of 200 Horse, comprising troops from various regiments and under the command of Colonel John Middleton. Urrey attacked the rear with about 1,000 horsemen just as Rupert with another 6,000 appeared on their flank over a crest by the modern-day Upham Farm, having travelled down what is today the A419. He did not have enough men to force a major battle but he did have sufficient to engage a portion of Essex's army, especially if it was strung out along its line of march.

The attack came near Dudmore Lodge, and it overwhelmed and scattered the rearguard and then followed them into the Parliamentarian column, taking them in flank and rear. The royal troopers caused panic and inflicted a number of casualties before Essex's infantry could group themselves around several small hillocks and the lower slopes of the valley; here two regiments formed improvised stands of pike and held them off. They were helped by parties of dragoons who got into the available cover and fired back, although they soon had a running skirmish on their hands with Royalist dragoons – presumably Rupert's own under Thomas Hooper.

Essex was frantically closing up his column and getting his army off the Downs and into the lanes and enclosures around Aldbourne when the Royalists attacked again, led by Colonel Urrey. With two regiments he slammed into the Parliamentarians but the accounts indicate he did not do as well as he ought to have done. Middleton fought back with two troops from the Earl of Denbigh's Regiment of Horse and another troop under Captain Wogan. Norton's and Hervey's Regiments of Horse joined in, followed by Grey's and Middleton's, supported by a party of commanded musketeers from Essex's own Regiment of Foot led by Captain Goland. Urrey was repulsed, and to retrieve the situation Lord Jermyn led the Queen's Regiment of Horse to his assistance. With great difficulty Sir Philip Stapleton, who commanded Essex's Regiment of Horse in the van, managed to halt and turn them, then worked his way back down the column to where the fight was happening. They met the Queen's with 'a volley of carabines . . . at lesse than ten yards' and the whole charge juddered, losing much of its momentum before it struck. Another party of Parliamentarians managed to wheel into the rear of the Queen's and there followed another large cavalry mêlée, into which Rupert took his own troop in order to extract Jermyn's men. Both sides

AN ALDBOURNE INCIDENT
The Marquis de Vieuville was a French ambassador sent by Louis XIV to negotiate peace between Charles I and Parliament. However, his romantic nature had caused him, alongside several others of his mission, to join Queen Henrietta Maria's service and to fight as 'reformados' (officers serving in the ranks). During the second phase of the battle, de Vieuville was at the head of the Queen's Regiment of Horse alongside its commanding officer Lord Jermyn and his friend Lord Digby, and the three of them charged at the senior enemy officer who was apparently commanding the body of Parliamentarian Horse the regiment had attacked. This lone officer fired his pistol at Digby's head. Luckily for Digby, the ball seems to have bounced off his helmet but he was stunned by the impact and blinded by the flash, albeit temporarily. Jermyn tried to run the enemy officer through the back but he too was saved by his armour, and then they were all swallowed up in the general fighting. The troopers of the Queen's Regiment tried to cut their way through the Parliamentarians rather than have to turn and fight their way back. During this mêlée de Vieuville's skull was crushed by a poleaxe wielded by Colonel Kilson and he was taken. Another account says he had bullet wounds in his chest, shoulder and face. The Parliamentarians took him to Hungerford, where he was attended by Essex's own surgeon, who operated on him to try to save his life, but he died of his terrible wounds. The next day, upon request, his body was returned to the King for an honourable burial, although some Royalist propaganda says the King had to pay for it, and indeed the Marquis was murdered.

suffered casualties until eventually Rupert realised he could not do any more damage to the retreating Parliamentarians and retired; his own horse was shot in the head but stayed alive long enough to get him off the battlefield. After a significant struggle in a hard-fought mêlée, Rupert's troopers relinquished their prey and withdrew, later revisiting the field and collecting two abandoned wagons that had overturned but were found to be still full of stores, ammunition and food.

The results of Aldbourne have been strangely played down in subsequent accounts of the first battle of Newbury, and it has been dismissed as a minor skirmish by many historians. Contrary to this view, I believe it had the crucial effect of delaying the Parliamentarian march, just as the Royalists needed. If Essex had pushed on south-eastwards, directly to Newbury, he could have reached his goal before the King, but he risked exposing his flank again, or even allowing Rupert to launch another attack. Having no idea that the main

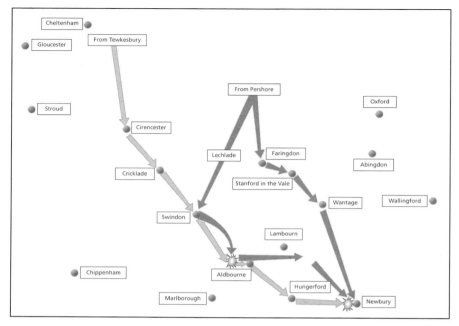

Map 5: After the feint northward, both sides raced for the Great West Road and the King sent Rupert with a flying column to harass and delay Essex's march.

Royalist army was still some distance away at Wantage, Essex supposed them to be at Lambourn and moved the Parliamentarian army southwards, away from where he thought his enemy to be. Given the restricted state of contemporary reconnaissance in general this was a very reasonable if not wise move, because it meant that he gained access not only to the main road but also to the bridge across the River Kennet at Hungerford. It would appear that he was intent on putting the Kennet on his left flank so that he could not be surprised again.

Peter Young and Richard Holmes state, 'For reasons which remain unexplained, Essex moved at a snail's pace on the 19th.' This casts some doubt on his abilities as a general. But as records show, Essex actually reached Hungerford at 6.00am and was then engaged in looking after the welfare of his army, allowing the medical teams to take care of the wounded and consolidating after Aldbourne. It would seem that he began his advance on Newbury soon enough, but because not all units in a large army can use the roads, some of his men had to cross the streams, marshes and wet ground in the Kennet Valley. The Great West Road would have been very useful for the majority of their wheeled transport, being south of the Kennet and therefore safer. The going was far more difficult, involving lots of short sharp gradients with brooks and hedges. The Royalists, however, were moving rapidly across the drier rolling chalk downs.

Even today, with the area drained to modern agricultural standards with a managed river and an eighteenth-century canal, it is still marshy in places and generally wet and soft underfoot. The summer of 1643 had been a wet one, and September had been a wet month despite the cold, frosty nights. The rivers were high and on the 19th more rain fell, turning the roads in the Kennet valley into muddy mires, bogging down men, guns and transport wagons alike. The Royalists in contrast were force-marching across the windswept uplands. As his men struggled through the miserable conditions, Essex sent news ahead for the people of Newbury to prepare for the arrival of his troops. Local legend has it that great preparations were made, with thousands of meals cooked and even decorations put up in the streets despite the rain. Essex's scouts and billeting officers reached Newbury from the west late that afternoon, but were suddenly surprised by several parties of royal Horse. These were also part of Rupert's 'flying column' command, which by this time had cut across the hypotenuse of the Aldbourne – Hungerford – Newbury triangle, and reached their goal at about the same time as Essex's quarter-masters and their escort. Pistol shots were exchanged and some fell to sword play until the sheer weight of numbers obliged the Parliamentarians to with-draw. This they did, leaving several men as prisoners and the cooked provisions in Royalist hands.

Learning that Newbury was now occupied by Royalists, Essex halted his army near Enborne, 2 miles west of the town, and on Crockham Heath he had the wet and weary soldiers make camp for the night. Some secondary accounts and Victorian maps have them lying down in order of battle; although likely, it is unsubstantiated. However, with the right wing protected by the Enborne River, often called the En Brook, and the baggage on the high ground east of Hamstead below Enborne Copse, they were secure; the 'official' Royalist account tells us the baggage was fenced with hedges and ditches and was inaccessible except by guarded defiles. Essex traditionally rode through the camp to the cry of 'Hey for Robin!' and later supposedly spent the night in a cottage belonging to a man called Biggs in the southern sector of the field. It seems rather distant from the centre of the army, but it was very convenient for examining the ground at close quarters.

The men slept in the open. By halting, Essex had allowed the royal infantry to catch up and the main body of Royalists reached Newbury that evening.

Despite the town's open hostility – there was a noted pro-Parliament community there – it was made to billet many senior officers. The Royalist headquarters appear to have been based in and around Cheap Street. The King himself lodged at the house of the mayor, Gabriel Cox(e), while his Secretary of State, Lucius Cary, Viscount Falkland, lodged with Mr Head and his family at no. 1. However, the quartermasters hurried the regiments through Newbury, not just because of the anti-Royalist disposition of many of the townspeople but to put the force into a position astride the Parliamentarians' direct route to London, which was now likely to bypass the town to the south, marching for Greenham, Aldermaston and Reading. The Royalists too settled down for the night tired and wet in the open on the slopes and high ground south-west of Newbury, in the area on either side of Wash Lane, which led up to Wash Common. There was some skirmishing, however, along the Enborne road.

Preparations for Battle

The King had finally achieved his strategic aim of getting his army across Essex's line of retreat and now Rupert sought a field upon which to offer the decisive tactical battle that would bring about the swift termination of the war. By chance he had found a suitable location among the enclosures and heathland to the south-west of Newbury, but it would appear that Charles was unwilling to force the issue, and although ready to fight if Essex obliged him to, he was not planning to force a general engagement. Although Rupert would perhaps have ridden over the soon-to-be-field, it seems Charles and his staff did not. No written or drawn battle deployment for either side has so far been discovered, and although having observed the ground, it would seem the Royalists formulated no plans on how best to employ it. We know, however, that Essex and his senior officers not only rode the ground but made a study of it as a potential battlefield. We have no drawings, no personal diary entries, but Essex's intention was to attack the next morning. He took stock of the ground before him.

Examining the lie of the land from the heights north of the modern Enborne road over to Red Heath and Broom Hill, Essex noticed a slope that rose from the water meadows of the River Kennet on his left up a series of spurs to substantial high ground on his right, only to drop away again rather steeply down to the En Brook – or the Enbourne or even the En River according to some old maps. In plan this higher area looks rather like a giant irregular oak leaf, with Monkey Lane, a road to London via Greenham, as its stalk. Royalist Horse seemed to be on the lower portions of the 'leaf' around Wash Common, and to have pushed westwards to the vicinity of Wash Common Farm, a little to the south of Round Hill, but the slopes to the south seemed unoccupied. Essex wanted that road to London. It would appear that with Newbury being both easily defensible and in Royalist hands, he decided only to threaten the town and the King's lines of communication. He chose to feint and hold with his left in the area of Guyer's Field, resting his flank on the Kennet, and to attack with his right on to Wash Common; it was to be a right hook to open a route to London. To make the plan work the whole army needed to pivot about its centre and the Parliamentarian officers saw the high ground to the south-east of Skinner's Green as the key to the action, especially one promontory that has become known as Round Hill and a lane that is now called Cope Hall Lane; this led directly to the northern common, Monkey Lane and the route to Reading and London. Essex might make the punch across the common, but Skippon had to hold the hill in order to feed over the baggage, the Reserve and Robartes' command. Cope Hall Lane, Wheatlands Lane and Enborne Street were essential transport routes which had to be taken, defended and utilised.

We have no way of telling from where Essex and his staff studied the field. It is probable that they rode north–south taking whatever opportunities any high ground offered. It is equally difficult today to gain easy access to that high ground, yet by driving along the several lanes or by walking the various footpaths between the hamlets of Enborne and Enborne Street, one can find a

The southern sector of the battlefield of Newbury from the Enborne Street flyover, showing the advance of Essex's Horse.

few reasonable vantage points, with the Newbury by-pass and its embankments both obscuring and facilitating modern views.

We can speculate on what Essex and his staff would have seen. They should have appreciated that the ground was rolling country offering few direct routes across the various spurs. There were also dense copses and innumerable banked hedges with ditches flanking fields and lining sunken lanes, which meant bodies of troops could move concealed from the enemy. However, these hedges also impeded deployed movement and the fighting styles both armies employed. The battlefield drills and minor tactics of both Foot and Horse required space and unimpeded ground to manoeuvre. Although nearer to Newbury itself the enclosures were more numerous and much smaller, the whole area was still criss-crossed by lanes. The more open fields of the northern sector were useful if not perfect, but formal battalion operations would be restricted in the centre and the south. However, it was splendid country for commanded muskets and dragoons, and for those officers who could fight with companies and troops rather than with regiments – those, in other words, who could make use of the enclosed ground by jamming lanes with pikemen, adopt lateral lanes as defensive fieldworks for musketeers and line approach hedges with dragoons. It would also suit those

A typical hedged lane. It was up roads like this that Essex's Horse advanced on to the common.

who understood combined arms, using infantry to secure or cut gaps in hedges and then provide a protective bridgehead or zone of fire cover for the cavalry to file through and deploy in the fields. With dragoons covering the flanks, the Horse would then advance and take the ground, holding it until the Foot, accompanied by light guns, could come up and take over. Organised effectively, such a combined arms force could make Essex's plan work.

During the campaign Essex had formed his army in battle array on a couple of occasions, notably at Brackley, Stowe and near Gloucester, and although he needed to make amendments to suit the enclosed nature of the ground at Newbury he and the senior officers would presumably have understood how time-consuming and complicated such manoeuvres would be. No deployment plan or battle order has yet been found but a lot of this information can be derived from the Parliamentarian colonels' account of the battle. It would seem that Essex had decided what he wanted to do even before many of his troops arrived in the area, for, if not in battle array, they were ordered to camp in position ready to attack the next day. He divided his army into two – one half to hold and the other to hook. He himself took command of the traditionally honourable right wing while the left was placed under Sergeant-Major General Philip Skippon. Lieutenant-General of Horse John Middleton had responsibility for the extreme left flank, but the majority of the Horse under Sir Philip Stapleton was attached to Essex. The Ordnance, consisting mainly of medium and light guns (the heavier pieces having been left to help defend Gloucester), was distributed to both wings, with most of the medium guns kept together in the centre.

Under his direct command Essex had three 'bodies of Foot', two brigades under Colonels Harry Barclay and James Holbourne and his own brigade-sized Lord General's Regiment. There is another sound argument based upon Foster's account that he also took the Red and Blue Regiments of the London Trained Bands. Some historians say they were on his right and led the attack, although it is doubtful he would have led with untried militia. His cavalry consisted of seven regiments of Horse, his own large Troop of Lifeguards and two companies of Dragoons. Skippon had three brigades of Foot, his own and those of Colonel John, Lord Robartes and Sergeant-Major General Randall Mainwaring, plus the unbrigaded regiment of Colonel Sir William Springate; perhaps Springate's was a 'double battalia' regiment like the Lord General's. Skippon also had a brigade of Horse commanded by Lieutenant-General John Middleton, and created a 'grand battery' out of the two heaviest guns in the army and perhaps the bigger of the light pieces. While Essex committed all his troops to his attack, for his holding force Skippon formed a Reserve with Mainwaring's Brigade, and drew out a substantial body of commanded muskets field-officered by Sergeant-Major Richard Fortescue, while his battery was assigned to increase the defensive firepower at the central hinge.

As Commander in Chief, Essex chose to place himself on the right and trusted Skippon to competently handle his centre and left wing. Essex's bravery and exemplary conduct under fire or in mêlée have never been in doubt but his battlefield awareness and grasp of a battle's ebb and flow have often been criticised. He took the usual post of a Commander, although to modern eyes his ability to exercise command and control over the whole field leaves much to be desired.

It would seem that the Royalists had no similar battle plan. Of course they would have had a battle order for the campaign but there is no evidence to suggest that they had ever drawn up or practised it. At the Council of War held on the evening of the 19th they decided to camp south of Newbury so as to be ready to deploy in the early morning, presumably in the prescribed battle order across Essex's route, if necessary. However, it seems there was a lack of deployment preparation: for example, Byron, commanding the van, occupied the centre rather than the right, and few Horse were initially posted on the right, even as a defensive measure. Perhaps they were satisfied with having successfully manoeuvred their forces between Essex and his London base. Even so, there must have been a discussion about the likelihood of battle, for Clarendon says that 'it was resolved over night not to engage in battle but upon such grounds as should give an assurance of victory'. However, no criteria for such grounds are noted, and it would appear that somebody determined that they would watch and wait. There is a view that Clarendon misjudged the situation and was writing from a position of 'political hindsight', but from a campaign perspective there appears to have been an idea that if Essex attacked, then the Royalists were to stop him, but how or where they were to do this seems to have been left to Rupert. Whether the Prince was informed of this responsibility is unknown, but regrettably for the King it would seem his nephew had neither general nor specific ideas regarding the suitability of the ground or his army's readiness, array or sequence of battle. Indeed, it becomes apparent – again through Lord Byron's and Clarendon's criticism – that although expecting to fight, the Royalist commanders, contrary to all good practice, formulated no particular plans for such an engagement. Clarendon lays the responsibility for the inaction at the feet of 'some young officers . . . who unhappily undervalued . . . the enemy, strong parties became successively so far engaged that the King was compelled to . . . battle'! However, it was more likely that Essex compelled the King to fight. In daylight the Royalists could see the importance of the high ground in the western part of Wash Common, particularly Round Hill. A large battery placed there could dominate the entire plateau of the common and play freely upon any troops trying to oppose a march across it. If the royal army was to prevent Essex from gaining the Reading Road and escaping to London they *had* to control Round Hill, otherwise they might as well retire to Oxford having failed in their

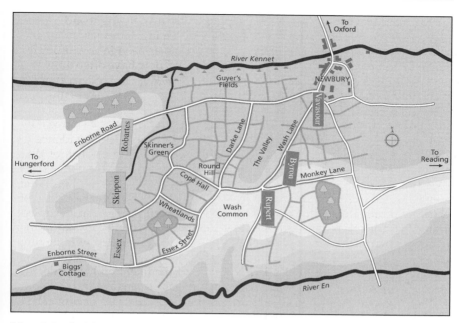

Map 6: Both sides arrayed themselves in three major bodies, although the Parliamentarians were better placed to achieve their aims.

strategic campaign aim. As the morning light revealed that Skippon had already occupied Round Hill, the Royalists had to respond and attack even though they had no predisposition to do so.

Although the Royalist response to Essex's attack was somewhat piecemeal, it must have borne some resemblance to the army battle order and there is some consistency among several Foot brigades with previous actions. Although we can never be certain, we can, by studying the accounts, determine a reasonable battle order. Commanding the right was Sir William Vavasour, with his own brigade of Foot and a small force of Horse. The centre was under Sir John Byron, who had part of his own brigade of Horse and his uncle Sir Nicholas Byron's Tertio of Foot (the Royalists tended to use the old-fashioned word tertio for brigade), as well as two bodies of commanded muskets under Sergeant-Major Generals Thomas, Lord Wentworth and George Lisle, and the Royalists' field-created own grand battery of artillery. Prince Rupert commanded the left and took to himself most of the army. He had Colonel John Belasyse's and Colonel Gilbert Gerard's Tertios of Foot and four brigades of Horse: his own and those of Colonel Charles Gerard, Colonel

Biggs' Cottage, where Essex supposedly spent the night before the battle.

Robert Dormer, Earl of Caernarvon, and Colonel Henry, Lord Wilmot; in addition he had the other part of Sir John's Byron's brigade of Horse as well, making five large bodies of Horse. According to period practice, the light and medium guns were probably spread along the line to accompany the Foot tertios.

As Commander in Chief of the Royalist Army, Charles Stuart seems sensibly to have remained in the centre and behind the lines, yet he too seems not to have exercised much overall command and control, although Foster has a tale of him riding about the royal lines dressed in a grey soldier's coat and bringing up both a regiment of Horse and one of Foot as well as firing two guns himself! This is all doubtful, but he was certainly there: Parliamentarian sources state their guns played without much success upon a group of bare-headed men, presumably in the royal presence. The royal standard is also said to have been flown on the common and there is a local legend that the King spent some of the battle in a hostelry that has since been rebuilt and become the Gun Inn, but any sort of proof is lacking. Despite the insistence of several historians that a few rudimentary entrenchments were thrown up, it would appear that neither Charles nor Rupert expected to fight. They knew Essex had camped in battle array but they seemed content with what they had achieved with their forced march across the downs. They naturally would have had scouts watching the Parliamentarians and some forward positions must have been held with a grand guard, but most of what was to be the battlefield high ground was unoccupied.

Essex, supposedly quartered in Biggs' Cottage, apparently spent a lot of the evening and night planning for the action, and it only remained to see how much of that unoccupied high ground his men could take before the royal command saw, understood and responded to what they were doing.

Essex Attacks

During the night several small cavalry skirmishes took place. During one such encounter Lord Percy was cut on the hand and Lord Jermyn had his helmet beaten in and was wounded near the eye. With the two armies lying so close to each other, it must have been a busy night for the pickets. Early in the morning of 20th September, well before dawn, the Parliamentarian army was roused and breakfasted, although Victorian tales of a roasted pig being blown from its spit by royal cannon shot are very far from likely! Before day-break the men had been assembled by regiment. They formed into what the Oxford

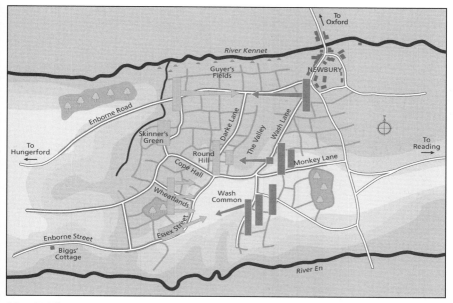

Map 7: The opening attacks and counter-measures made by both sides, although Rupert's Horse may have avoided the gully.

Account describes as 'three bodies of Foot, both lined and flanked with strong bodies of Horse', and began their march towards the Royalist lines. Presumably these were the three main infantry commands of Essex, Skippon and Robartes. Depending upon the field view of the observer, the 'Grand Reserve', as Digby described it, at Skinner's Green could have been interpreted as part of either Skippon's or Robartes' command – it certainly was posted to cover both.

Essex's body, or wing, was the first to move. The majority of the troops made their way south-east from Crookham Heath probably in two columns, one of Horse and the other of Foot, all the time heading for Wash Common, with the central Wheatlands Lane being used for the accompanying light guns. If Essex had slept at Biggs' Cottage to the south, he would have already had part of his force near him and these men would presumably have been some night flank units of horse which advanced up the southernmost lane towards the open common. Although some historians believe this lane to be too far south, it may well have been the route for some of Stapleton's cavalry on the right flank of the army.

It would have been necessary for Stapleton's Horse to ride up this lane in

The approximate location where Enborne Street met Wash Common and perhaps the gap through which Stapleton's men debouched on to the open land.

compacted groups, but by leaving the Foot to advance separately they should have been less able to clear the flanking hedges and would have lacked supporting firepower for any trouble they might encounter. However, Essex's troopers seem to have had little difficulty in dislodging the Royalist scouts and skirmishers, and secured a small bridgehead on the common. Stapleton's leading regiments, Essex's own double-sized Troop of Lifeguard and his Regiment of Horse apparently reached the end of the lane where enclosures gave way to scrubland and debouched from track and fields on to the plateau at the southern end of Wash Common and arrayed themselves in line, supported by Dalbier's Regiment of Horse. Each troop of approximately sixty troopers was arrayed in three squadrons, line abreast, with each squadron consisting either of three files of six (the Dutch system) or six files of three (the Swedish). This short line probably ran north-west/south-east with its right upon a deep gully.

Stapleton adhered to the established theory of first weakening the enemy with carbine and pistols and then dispersing the shot-shattered formation with the sword. The Royalists had not been inactive and had by that time established a cavalry guard on that hill, too. How large it was we are not told but it seems to have been big enough to launch an attack on the Parliamentarian Horse, its front constricted by the gully. Stapleton's troopers stood and fired their pistols at close range, avoiding the folly of firing too soon (the mistake that undid Ramsey's command at Edgehill). The Royalist attack faltered and the Parliamentarians went at them with the sword, driving them off and chasing them back to where they had come from. Dalbier and Copely were wounded in this action, but after scattering the enemy Stapleton's men rallied and returned in good order to their start point, where the rest of Essex's attack force had now assembled, occupying ground from Wash Common Farm to the area of Enborne Lodge. Having marched up the slopes, they started to push their way through or climb over the hedges lining the common, re-forming on a north–south line approximately where the modern Essex Street turns into Enborne Street today. Some of the infantry are supposed to have taken a more direct route to the rendezvous, apparently climbing Wheatlands Hill east of Long Copse, thus taking more unoccupied high ground, and bringing them out on to open ground to form up with the rest of the wing. Once reformed, Essex's body was ready for its next task of driving across Wash Common and turning the Royalists' left flank.

Meanwhile Skippon too had set off early from Crockham Heath and made rapid progress across the fields and the lane up the northernmost hill, today called Cope Hall Lane. Apart from small pickets, his leading units of commanded musketeers under Sergeant-Major Richard Fortescue met no serious opposition and surprisingly easily took possession of the crucial central Round Hill and both the lanes that were to be the pivot and the arteries respectively of the battle plan. From this vantage point Skippon could see the enemy army assembling and deploying, and so ordered his own regiments out of marching column and into battle formation.

Understanding the time line of the battle is difficult but it would appear that Skippon held back his left until the enemy guns opened fire. He probably would have preferred not to have the left deploy forward at all, but it is likely that the Royalist movement towards the Kennet Valley provoked him into sending the brigade of Colonel John, Lord Robartes to the left, towards the Kennet, supported by Colonel John Middleton's Brigade of Horse. They took time but had an unhindered advance first to and then along the Enborne Road. Having gained possession of the small enclosed fields both in the centre and to his right, Skippon established his holding position. On the left Robartes' men began lining the hedges with musketeers, securing the lanes and any gaps with pikemen and supporting them in the fields both to the rear and to the flank with heavy horse, thereby effectively sealing off the route of any Royalist attempt to march directly westward out of Newbury to outflank the Parliamentarian line. In the centre Skippon must have found a far better position than he could have wished for! Between the rising ridge on which the royal army had camped and the now secure Parliamentarian Round Hill lay a deep depression; the high ground to the east of this depression is sometimes called the Escarpment, while some locals refer to the dip more accurately as 'the valley'. Lining the hedges that over-looked this valley with 1,000 musketeers drawn from the regiments of the Bristol garrison, under Sergeant-Major Richard Fortescue, Skippon then brought up and deployed his own brigade of Foot with two small pieces of artillery as well as Springate's Regiment to support them; they too made good use of the banked hedge systems.

As soon as he had seen what a good arc of control the Round Hill enjoyed, Skippon commanded Merrick to order the Parliamentarian Trayne and its accompanying pioneers to haul the largest of the guns up Cope Hall Lane in preparation either to take advantage of the commanding position or for the march to Reading. He also ordered the Reserve, Sergeant-Major General Randall Mainwaring's City of London Brigade of Foot, to commence its march and come up to the rear of the hill near the houses of Skinner's Green. The right hook was beginning to take shape. Having taken their first objectives and strengthened their positions, the Parliamentarian commanders and their men now awaited the Royalist army's reaction.

Rupert Responds

Essex's advance surprised the Royalists and in the early morning light Rupert found his army desperately trying to form up with a formed foe on their flank. The situation was dangerous. Something had to be done to prevent the

Parliamentarians advancing further and destroying the royal army as it marched into position. It seems Rupert decided to both contain Essex in the more open ground of the southern sector and make a strong demonstration to hold Skippon in the enclosures in the centre. About 5.00am he issued orders to the vanguard of Horse. Having appropriated part of it for his own command, presumably deeming it more immediately useful in the south, he ordered Sir John Byron to take the rest of his brigade forward against the Round Hill and to support an attack upon it led by Wentworth's and Lisle's commanded muskets. He was only to take two regiments of Horse, his own and that of Sir Thomas Aston, and they were to draw up behind the musketeers and 'be ready to second them in case the enemy's horse should advance towards them'. Then, taking much of the Horse with him, he hurried to the left to confront Essex. We can only surmise that he was not expecting a general engagement and thus hurried to the point of most imminent danger, leaving the rest of the deployment action to his subordinates.

The Royalist accounts are critical of Rupert and show some admiration for Essex. They say that the Parliamentarian general led Rupert into attacking him in a strong position by offering him the prospect of an apparently easy victory in the south if he could muster enough Horse. Clarendon describes the battle as one which grew out of a series of small engagements begun by brave royal officers in localised command who could not appreciate the bigger picture. Once engaged, they had to be reinforced or be broken, and such reinforcements led to the whole army gradually being drawn in to a major battle of the sort they had hoped to avoid; or, as Clarendon put it, 'the King was compelled to put the whole of a hazard of a battle, and to give the enemy at least an equal game to play'. This was not a set-piece battle for the Royalists but a series of events leading to a steady escalation of commitment.

On the Royalist left the first attack had been repulsed and now, with Rupert having arrived, the second attack was about to go in. Three bodies of Foot plus supporting light guns, lined and flanked with Horse, was a classic combined-arms defensive tactic, especially on a front narrowed by the gully. The musketeers and cannon could volley at long range to bring down enemy troopers, and then add their fire to the shorter-range carbine and pistol shot from the interlarded Horse. The muskets were protected by their pikemen, whose own vulnerable flanks were, in turn, protected by the swords of the cavalry troopers who could spur forward to absorb a degree of enemy impetus. The whole formation also had dragoon fire support, probably concealed in the flanking hedges. If overrun, the gunners could shelter among the pikemen and if beaten in mêlée, individual troops of horse could withdraw behind the blocks of Foot to re-form and reorder. (Interestingly, reloading did not seem to be part of the process, perhaps because fresh Horse had arrived.)

Ramsey's, Harvey's and Goodwin's forces, along with three troops under Luke, had come through the gap on to the Common and deployed to meet Rupert, who now led his fresh regiments forward 'with all possible haste'. The gully may have forced both sides to concentrate so the Royalists became good targets and could not deploy their superior numbers. The steep incline probably prevented Rupert hooking Stapleton's line, although his men successfully fought up steeper hills at Lansdown. The combination of long-range musket and short-range pistol firepower, protected flanks and a determination to engage the Royalists in mêlée enabled Stapleton's Brigade to drive off Rupert's second attack and the Royalists were once again forced back across the common. However, many of the Parliamentarian troopers were now unloaded, especially the Lifeguard, Essex's and Dalbier's regiments who had been in action twice.

Rupert regrouped and his Horse went forward again. Stapleton had also reformed but this time the Parliamentarian fire was less plentiful and the third attack went in without too many preliminary casualties. Fighting a break-out action, Stapleton was also outflanked, so some made it up the slope, and Rupert's units were now sufficiently numerous to attack him in both front and flank. Clarendon recounts that they did so 'with a kind of contempt for the enemy' and that they were unequalled, boldly charging and 'far too hard for the troops on the other side that they routed them in most places'. This suggests that fresh troops of Horse had come up who were minus the 'respect' of those who had been previously driven back. Which regiments made the first, second or third attack we cannot tell, but Rupert had part of Byron's brigade, plus Gerard's, Caernarvon's, Wilmot's and his own Horse on that wing. One is tempted to think that Sir Samuel Sandys' regiment, which had been part of Byron's Brigade, had been thrown into the second attack.

It would appear that this successive feeding-in of units reaped its rewards on the south side of the common. Outnumbered and out of shot, Stapleton's tired brigade crumbled and the men were forced back before the determined Royalist onslaught. Pushed back, many sought to get behind their Foot, while others looked to escape through gaps in the hedges lining the Common; many were forced to go back via the lanes and tracks that had given them entry to the open ground. It was a drawn-out, confused general mêlée in which the Parliamentarian captains Hammond, Fleetwood and Pym were wounded, and Captain Draper 'behaved himself very gallantly'. Several parties of Royalists pursued the fleeing troops into the lane, trying to cut their foes down from the rear. These pursuers were apparently all either shot down by Abercromby's and/or Shibborne's dragoons who, from the safety of their embanked hedgerows, would have been firing at point-blank range, or dragged from their mounts and stabbed to death by the Foot. A similar fate

The remains of Wash Common's once-thick western boundary hedge, to which Essex's Foot retired and made their stand.

awaited those who chased after those troopers who fled down Wheatlands Lane. Money records a local tradition that the Royalists pursued their fleeing foes towards Enborne and that the lane between that village and Skinner's Green was so clogged with the dead of both sides that a passage had to be cleared before it could be used again. It is obviously an exaggeration. Despite the losses of these small parties who pursued too far, Rupert's success seemed guaranteed; having driven off Stapleton's Brigade, his troopers could now left-hook across the gully, turn the line of the Foot and force them back to the hedges lining the common. Rupert had stopped Essex and captured five pieces of artillery, even managing to drag one away as a trophy, but his success came at a price. Foster records that the Parliamentarians took three cornets and a piece of another! However, despite the bravery of their cavalry, the Royalists could not break Essex's infantry.

Several charges were made and the Parliamentarians gave ground, probably falling back to the hedge that lined the common or even down the slope, but it is difficult to envisage how the Royalist horse got control of the first enclosures on these slopes when all the evidence about cavalry in hedged country militates against this happening? It is more likely that without Horse to protect their flanks Essex's Foot was forced to make a fighting retirement, giving ground stubbornly and falling back to make use of the ditched hedge that marked the western boundary of the common; presumably the dragoons also gave them covering fire. The combined pressure from Horse and Foot pushed them off the common but they bought enough time for their own Horse to retreat without being broken. Clarendon had to admit that 'the Foot behaved themselves admirably . . . and gave their Horse time to rally'. Exactly where Stapleton's Horse rallied is not clear but it seems to have been some-where in the vicinity of the modern A34 dual carriageway at the eastern foot of Boames/Biggs Hill. One school of thought maintains that the Foot fell back to Skinners' Green Lane. Looking at both the old and the more modern lanes of that name, one might envisage the cavalry going that far, but placing the Foot there too at this stage tends to work against the evidence offered by the story of the London Trained Bands, although it could just work on the ground. By nightfall it looks likely that Stapleton, who had worn out three horses with the day's exertions, had his brigade ready to go forward yet again. Whether they moved forward to the slight rise to the west of Enborne Street where Trundle and Wheatlands Hills merge is unknown; it is certainly possible. Wherever they went, they played no further part in the action other than to act as cavalry support and pose a threat that would not go away.

With Rupert's men pinning his force behind their hedge, Essex's attack across Wash Common to take the London Road had come to a grinding stop. However, his battered wing was not beaten yet. The best of the Royalist horse had defeated the best of his Horse, but they had not run as many had done at Edgehill and they were busily regrouping behind his steadfast Foot. Rupert may have gained the upper hand on the southern part of the field but he had not won it. He had not turned Essex's flank and there seemed little possibility of him doing so.

BATTLEFIELD INCIDENTS
During this third clash Bulstrode relates how Sir Philip Stapleton rode out in front of his Horse into a small knot of Royalist officers, where he sought out Prince Rupert and fired his pistol at his head. The Prince was saved by his helmet and Stapleton turned his horse and returned to his station, despite the numerous pistol balls flying about his own head. Stapleton's groom too had an adventure. His horse having been killed under him, he struggled back to his own lines on foot – only to return into the fray to collect his saddle and bridle, which were new. He is said to have waded back into the fighting to retrieve his property despite the 'hundreds of bullets [that] flew about his ears'.

Central Counter-attacks

In the centre Sir John Byron's troops were first deployed to the west of the modern Wash Lane facing westward, and then moved forward on to the slopes overlooking a fairly deep valley. Byron understood that not occupying Round Hill was a grievous oversight and his first move was to try to take it. He ordered a move forward but, despite getting over the valley and up to the hedges that lined the crest on the far side, Wentworth's and Lisle's commanded musketeers could not dislodge their counterparts ensconced on the elevated ground, especially as Fortescue's line had Skippon's own brigade and its two pieces of light artillery to support it. He therefore called for his uncle, Sir Nicholas Byron, to commit his brigade of Foot and reinforce Wentworth and Lisle. They took the first hedge-line, forcing Fortescue's men to fall back across some open land, possibly an enclosure, to another hedge, where the attack continued.

Initially three regiments pushed forward and all suffered severe casualties. Colonel Charles Gerard's Regiment of Foot appears to have borne the brunt of the action, reporting afterwards that they had lost Edward Villiers, their lieutenant-colonel (who was shot in the shoulder), two captains, four lieutenants, nine ensigns, seven sergeants and seventy-nine soldiers. It is also believed that the Prince of Wales's Regiment under Sir Michael Woodhouse was also hotly engaged and met with great ferocity – possibly in revenge for the atrocities they had committed on unnamed prisoners after the capture of

COMMANDED MUSKETS

When fighting in enclosed country pike blocks were difficult to handle and of limited use, so commanders used to 'draw out' parties of musketeers, detaching them from their regiments and sending them forward to engage in firefights, under a temporarily nominated commanding officer. Like the dragoons, such parties made the best use possible of any available cover. It is interesting to note that at Newbury I both sides used large parties of commanded musketeers, and in fact both Wentworth and Lisle held the rank of Sergeant-Major General of Dragoons. Fortescue had also commanded dragoons. It may be that rather than being drawn from the Foot regiments, the commanded muskets at Newbury were the 'dragooners' of both sides, holding and clearing hedges until the Foot came up. In 1643 many dragoons still carried muskets, as did the Foot, although they were changing over to snaphaunce locks, the lighter carbine being reserved for use on horseback, by the Parliamentarians at least.

The scrub hedge from which the Royalists drove Fortescue's commanded muskets and continued their attack across the open ground.

Hopton Castle. At one point, however, the Royalist attack seems to have stalled and the cry went up for Horse to second them. This might seem unusual given the enclosed ground but they were losing the firefight and needed mêlée troops to take the defended hedge-line. Byron moved his two regiments of Horse forward and then rode up to see what they could do. His view was not promising, especially as the compacted chalk surface running between the remains of two grubbed-out hedges suggests strongly that this was a farm lane and would have been quite a substantial obstacle. This was most probably the hedged track known as Darke Lane; it was lined with musketeers and even had light cannon thrust through it. It was on the plateau of land that must have appeared to be the eastern slope of Round Hill and was both high and thick, and virtually impassable to Horse. It must have seemed hopeless until Byron espied a narrow gap, just wide enough for a single trooper to force his way through. He issued orders to widen the gap and then had his horse shot from under him with bullets in the throat and mouth. As he called for a remount a volunteer trooper rode at the gap and cut his way through, only to be immediately shot and killed. This brave man was Lucius Cary, Viscount Falkland, Charles I's Principal Secretary of State. There are several romantic stories attached to Falkland's heroics but militarily his corpse and that of his dead steed gained a tiny foothold through which others could follow, buying enough time for men to hack back the foliage and widen the gap. It must have been a desperate business but eventually there was room to get several troopers through. Byron struggled forward with his own troop of Horse and sent a somewhat disordered frontal charge at the Parliamentarian ranks. They were met 'with a great salvo of musket shot, and . . . two drakes . . . laden with case shot which killed some and hurt many of my men'. They were forced to wheel off and could not complete the charge to contact.

Nevertheless they too had bought more time and the gap in the hedge grew wider, and more Royalists poured through it, flooding into the lane. Seeing this enemy build-up on its flank, the Parliamentarian line gave ground; dragging their guns with them, the men tried to retire across the enclosure, down a slight dip to yet another hedge. Byron kept the pressure on and advanced after them, this time with Sir Thomas Aston's Regiment involved too, hoping to cut them up before they reached the hedge. They were successful in routing or killing most of those they caught in the enclosure, but those who reached the new hedge now had the pikes of the second line reaching over their heads and the second line musketeers standing on the banks lending their fire to the

Darke Lane as it crests the rise before Round Hill. Somewhere in this vicinity was the gap through which Falkland forced his horse, only to be killed in the attempt.

defence. Once again the attack was obliged to wheel away, and although some horsemen did get to the hedge and into a mêlée, when the majority pulled off the Parliamentarians used the opportunity to scramble over and through the hedge to safety. Meanwhile more Royalist Foot began the fight yet again but this hedge was too high, too thick and too well manned to be overcome; despite this, their efforts did allow the Horse to withdraw, possibly to the cover of the valley.

The fight at the hedge eventually lost momentum and Nicholas Byron's men pulled back to the double hedge and then brought up their own light guns to help them. At some point in the afternoon a party of Parliamentarian musketeers came up the lane and threatened their right flank and right rear. This may have been late in the day and the musketeers from the Red Auxiliaries, but it is also possible that they were men from Springate's Regiment of Foot who had wheeled across and up the slope. Sir Thomas Aston took his own troop down the lane to drive them off. His horse was shot under him and Aston was unable to free his leg from the stirrup before the panicking animal dragged him into the midst of the enemy. Only after his horse collapsed was he able to extricate himself; he regained the Royalist lines on foot.

Round Hill from the site of the erstwhile double-hedged lane. The dip between the two parts of the high ground is clear, as is the third hedge and the open rise where Skippon had Merrick place his battery.

The lane running north towards the Enborne road and Robartes' position. Up here came the body of musketeers that Aston dispersed.

Taking Round Hill was proving a difficult task. Skippon's Brigade had been driven back off the first rise, but they still held the all-important hill. The Royalists' single-enclosure bridgehead on Round Hill had been achieved at a high cost. In addition to the losses among Wentworth's and Lisle's men, as well as those in Nicholas Byron's and Aston's Brigades, Byron recalled that he 'lost near upon a hundred horse and men, out of my regiment, whereof out of my own troop twenty-six'. A lull now settled over the centre.

The North Holds

Of the known accounts, none was written by a person who fought all day on the northern flank, so although the King's standard was seen here we have to rely upon snippets and deductions. We know that Skippon's intention was to prevent a flanking movement by any Royalist forces from the direction of Newbury itself, for not only would this have turned Essex's left flank, it would also have opened a direct route to his baggage gathered on the slopes below Enborne Chase. To prevent this disaster he had to block the 'the high way that came Newbury just upon us'. Skippon sent Colonel John, Lord Robartes' Brigade of Foot and four drakes (light guns) to do that job and presumably covered its open left flank and rear with regiments of Horse from Colonel John Middleton's Brigade – although there is not much evidence to back this assumption. The guns were evidently placed on the road and 'well defended', which could mean that a lateral barricade of sharpened branches between the thick hedges was constructed too. It was a prudent move, as working its way towards that flank was Colonel-General Sir William Vavasour's Brigade of Foot, which, although we do not have full details of its composition, is believed to have been a very strong body, including several unlisted Welsh regiments. He also had with him some cavalry support, although nothing to rival Colonel Middleton's Brigade of Horse which might have awaited them. There is a suggestion that Middleton had a much more complicated brief than merely covering Robartes' Brigade and that the constituent units of his command were widely dispersed, first to guard against any Royalist encirclement of the extreme left, thus protecting the baggage and the rear of the whole army, and safeguarding its possible route in the event of an enforced retreat, and secondly to rearguard the anticipated advance to Round Hill and the two lanes, followed by the withdrawal of Skippon's Brigade and the army's crossing of the common and the march for Reading.

Vavasour's 'forlorn hope' was the first to attack, exchanging fire with Robartes' men; in this skirmish Robartes' lieutenant-colonel was hit in the face. However, the Parliamentarian light guns also opened up, presumably at close range, and the Royalists abandoned their positions and ran. The Parliamentarians occupied the ground as Vavasour's full body came up. Skippon probably saw them from his commanding position on Round Hill for he dispatched Fortescue and his more mobile units to join Robartes to help counter this threat; he was perhaps reluctant to send any of the more cumbersome Foot regiments in any direction other than towards the battle objective of turning and slipping round the south flank. Although we cannot be sure, Fortescue is likely to have moved once the central Parliamentarian line was established in the second line of enclosures, and the fighting changed from the work of commanded muskets to the combined fire and mêlée tactics more suited to Skippon's own brigade of mixed-arm Foot. Fortescue's force apparently arrived in time to take a position left of Robartes' men, actually upon and across the road into Guyer's Fields, although this would have meant getting among the guns. Some historians say Middleton's Brigade moved at the same time, but this seems rather late to perform the standard practice of placing cavalry on the wing to cover the end of the line. Why the fighting on the northern flank began later in the day is rather a mystery. Perhaps it was just a question of distance, being further to march for both sides, but it could be that Robartes was reluctant to get too engaged if he was awaiting orders to fall back and then withdraw over Round Hill once the baggage and the Reserve had gone. One result of the realignment was that the most flexible and mobile Foot forces were transferred to the infantry position with the furthest to travel if the order came to march away; moreover, being supported by several light guns to help stem any pursuit, they could also help move them, for no army left guns behind if it could be avoided.

No matter the reasons for the late start, the engagement when it came was still bloody. At one point the Royalists actually got among Robartes' guns and dragged off one of their limbers, although its capture was 'with the loss of many of their lives'. The enclosed nature of much of the ground on either side of the road meant that each hedge-line had to be won if Vavasour's attack was to gain ground. According to Rocque's map, the ground around the Enborne Road seemed more open and better suited to Middleton's Horse, but it seems to have proved otherwise. Vavasour's men, although protected by the east–west hedges, could not venture across them for fear of being cut down, their Horse support being too small to be effective. In fact, both sides were limited to small parties fighting for gaps in hedges. The only tactic for the majority of Vavasour's force was thus a head-on assault, which was costly. Who ordered the transfer we do not know, but Wentworth's and Lisle's commanded

The Enborne road. Somewhere along here Robartes resisted Vavasour's attack and then launched his attempted counter-attack.

muskets now moved, like Fortescue's, from the centre to this northern sector via a lane on the reverse slope and so found themselves engaged with their foes in a similar battle for hedge-lines. To counter this, Skippon drew out 'sixty files of musketeers' (360–400 men) from his Reserve at Skinner's Green and sent them to join the fighting, which they did, positioning themselves to the right of Robartes. Again it is worth noting these were not full regiments and did not include the slower pikemen.

It is interesting at this stage to look at the role of Sergeant-Major General Randall Mainwaring's Regiment of Foot. Officially part of the London Brigade in the Reserve, it too seems to have been committed to this wing and was sent forward to fill the gap between Robartes' men and Round Hill, coming up on the left of Springate's independent regiment. This anchored Springate's flank and allowed him to perform a battlefield wheel, which was quite a feat. It appears that he swung his regiment through 45 degrees and marched up the slope of the hill to threaten Byron's flank if he dared move forward again, co-incidentally also aiming at the common and the route home.

Back in the northern hedges, the royal troops fired, advanced, fired and charged; however, met by volley after volley, they were eventually forced to retire. Sometimes the fighting must have been butt against butt or have come to push of pike over the hedges, but despite everything Vavasour's Brigade could hurl at them, Robartes' men did not give ground. Several historians claim that Vavasour's attack was not pressed home with any great ardour; however, his men do seem to have got into the Parliamentarian line so the effort must have been there at some stage. No matter how hard the Royalists attacked, the Parliamentarians held their bloodied hedge, and secured the northern flank.

Towards evening it seems that, perhaps encouraged by a lull, or by news that the breakthrough on the right had been halted and that overall the battle had not gone according to plan, Robartes tried a counter-attack, which seems to have reached as far as Guyer's Lane, described as 'a passe by the river', which ran north from the Enborne Road down to the Kennet, only to be thwarted by the arrival of more Royalist Horse. According to Digby, this was His Majesty's Lifeguard Regiment of Horse, whom Stuart had taken over to the right as a reserve or, some say, to counter Middleton's numbers. This is confusing as they had supposedly begun the day with Rupert on the left. Perhaps their status and their abilities made them more suited to acting as a mobile reserve rather than being committed to attacking Essex's Foot entrenched behind the hedges of Wash Common. Even the arrival of these prestigious troops did not influence the basic situation. Robartes still held his flank and could not be shifted.

Crisis

Despite the initial set-back, it seems that Essex's Foot with its light guns moved slowly but steadily forward, all the time encouraged by Essex waving a distinctive white hat and crying, 'Forward, bravehearts!' They were gradually gaining the vital ground that opened the door to the London road. Alas, that ground to the east of Enborne Street is now built over, but the ridge of flat land is clearly visible.

It appeared that there was little Rupert's Horse could do against this large-scale attack in the southern sector as its firepower was too strong. But Rupert was not prepared to give up. He had Colonel John Belasyse's and Colonel Gilbert Gerard's Tertios of Foot march to support him, possibly along what is now the Andover Road, and then committed them both – although Belasyse's men on the left of the line seem to have borne the brunt of the work. Again we lack details of the action but the Parliamentarians recorded that they were 'hotly charged by the enemies' horse and foot'. The fighting here too must have been bloody for we are told that it spanned four hours and the Royalists steadily gained ground, forcing their foes back on to the edge of the common. Colonel Charles Gerard's Brigade of Horse must have been seriously involved in these attacks for they were so badly cut up and broken that they were obliged to retire to the rear and re-form. Still not broken, Essex clung to his grip on the high land. His detractors suggest he feared he might be broken and wanted reinforcements, but his call to Skippon for more men could equally be interpreted as a desire to maintain or renew the pressure so as to stick to his objective of turning the Royalist flank. He was certainly maintaining a steady build-up of troop numbers in the southern sector.

Skippon's answer was to take the men of Mainwaring's Regiment out of his front line on the left and send them across, with their place being taken by the Blue Regiment of the City of London Auxiliaries. They were marched over, presumably moving round the west of Round Hill to somewhere near the entrance to Wheatlands Lane. Keith Roberts in his book *The First Battle of Newbury, 1643* says Skippon may have been unsure of the fighting capabilities of the Trained Bands and Auxiliaries and so chose the most experienced London regiment for this reinforcement task; however, yet again we see evidence of the regiments being shifted south. However, even their experience could not counter the storm they met, for no sooner did they begin replacing some of Essex's exhausted infantry than they were charged by two great bodies of Horse and assailed by Foot, although the latter seemed less than enthusiastic. These were probably Wilmot's and the southern part of Byron's Brigades, in conjunction with regiments from Gerard's Tertio. The activities of the Royalist Horse would have obliged the musketeers to seek protection from the pikemen, thus allowing the infantry attack to go in almost unopposed. Whatever happened, Mainwaring's men were quickly overrun and forced to retreat, giving up the precious ground that Essex's men had seized earlier and had so stubbornly clung to. Strangely, the Royalist Foot did not press home their advantage, seemingly content with having pushed the Parliamentarians off the common, which their commander Belasyse cites as a laudable achievement. Despite the men's exhaustion, Essex's line launched a counter-attack led by Barclay's Brigade, which gave 'a round salvo', presumably a full battalia volley, with every musketeer firing at the same time. Holbourne's and Essex's own brigades advanced yet again and retook the ground, apparently forming yet another line along the banked and hedged common-side lane, ready to go once more if the opportunity presented itself.

However, their losses and the retreat of Mainwaring's men had opened up a serious gap in the Parliamentarian line at the juncture of the two wings of the army. If Rupert could drive into and through this opening he would pierce Essex's centre, break the two wings apart and be able to fall upon their rear.

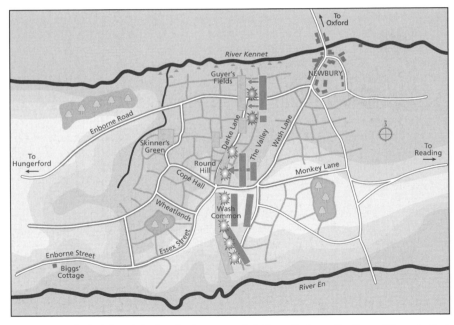

Map 8: At the height of the battle there was fighting all along the line, although that in the south may have been compressed much further north.

He smartly began redeploying his brigades. His own, Caernarvon's and Wilmot's Horse with Belasyse's Foot would contain Essex, while Charles Gerard's Brigade of Horse and Gilbert Gerard's Brigade of Foot would drive through the gap and secure victory. Not having reconnoitred the ground, Rupert was not to know that a major cavalry push through the centre would be very difficult because of the steep nature of the slopes they would encounter beyond the hilltop enclosures.

However, here we come to a problem. Views differ according to how one reads the accounts of two participants, Foster of the Red Regiment and an unidentified soldier in the Blue Regiment. One school of thought puts these two units with Essex, while the other school puts them with the Reserve. The latter is the more widely accepted interpretation, but nobody is yet in a position to say which is correct – although protagonists will lobby strongly for their version. In the absence of proof, I have opted for the following version, although it is offered with some trepidation!

Luckily for the Parliamentarians, Skippon saw the dangerous opening and ordered the Red Regiment and the Blue Regiment of the London Trained Bands forward to close it. It appears that they marched from the enclosed area

The site of the Royalist battery in Falkland Recreation Ground and the direction in which the guns fired; just beyond the trees is Blossom Field.

of Skinner's Green, up Cope Hall Lane, the way Essex always intended the Reserve to go, then across to the right to just below the northern end of Wash Common, where they took up their position in the line, re-forming the link between the sections of the army. The Red Regiment was furthest north and so had the Blue on its right. Today this area is occupied by Wash Common Farm and its fields, while beyond Enborne Street there is another field (Blossom Field) and some woods surrounding the water tower, but in 1643 all this was described as 'open campania'. There was no cover and they were to suffer for it. On the high ground before them, in the top west corner of the common, the Royalists had drawn up a grand battery of eight heavy guns, well protected by both Foot and Horse and at such short range that Sergeant Foster of the Red Regiment estimated it at 'far lesse than twice musket shot'. The site of this battery is often ascribed to the ground around the Falkland Memorial opposite the Gun Inn; this might well have been on the battery's right flank but the ground suggests that the guns were set at an angle across what is now Falkland Recreation Ground, endeavouring to obtain a direct line of fire on to Round Hill (but avoiding Byron's troops). Presented with the nearer and more immediate target of two close-formation militia regiments, they opened up on the Londoners.

Blossom Field east of Wash Common Farm. Here the London regiments stood their ground under close-range artillery fire.

Although the angles dictate that the Londoners could not have taken the fire from all eight pieces, theirs must have been the most desperate situation any unit found itself in that day. Ordered to plug the gap, they could not move, not even to advance. In open ground they had to endure close-range battery fire from heavy guns, 'when men's bowels and brains flew in our faces', and resist attacks from both Horse and Foot. Being on the left, the Red Regiment had the worst of it. Two regiments of Royalist Horse from the right flank of the guns charged them early in the action, but were met by a desperate volley that 'made them flie'. Later another party charged the Blue Regiment but here too the men gave fire 'with so much violence and success that they sent them now not wheeling but reeling'. In spite of these successes, the temptation to retire or even run must have been great, but stand they did, 'blessed be to God that gave us courage'. Brave, bloodied and unbowed as they were, the amount of artillery shot was bound to tell eventually. Skippon had to do something about it. By this time the guns he had ordered earlier that day to be hauled up Round Hill had arrived under the command of Sir John Merrick. It is likely that Essex never intended them to be deployed but rather kept moving across the hill and over the common heading for Reading, but Skippon was now obliged to use them. He had them align in battery, like the Royalist guns, but they were placed so they could support both Skippon's defence of the hill and the hard-pressed Londoners. Colonel Tucker from the Red Regiment went to some light guns to encourage them to come to the aid of his men, and succeeded in actually directing and firing one piece, but upon helping to lay it for a second shot he was struck in the head by an enemy cannon ball.

In the face of these frequent and determined attacks on the two Trained Band units, the Parliamentarian centre was in jeopardy. Determined the Londoners might be, but they were still militia and they had not seen action before. If they broke, Skippon's line, consisting of his own brigade and his newly placed battery, would be outflanked and rolled up. Skippon called up more of the Reserve from Skinner's Green, bringing them into action but maintaining the strategic aim of having them ready to march across Round Hill and then the common. This time it was the turn of the Red Regiment of the City of London Auxiliaries to come up on to the hill where Skippon deployed them to the left of the guns. He also covered the open right flank of Merrick's battery with files of musketeers from his own experienced regiment to make the best of a worrying situation. The guns then opened up at short range in open country: at that distance they could hardly miss and they 'did very good execution'. However, it was too late for the two militia regiments. Losses and constant fighting had thinned their ranks and the two units were obliged to merge in order to remain a cohesive ordered body and effect a fighting retreat to the southern slopes of Round Hill. Some of them withdrew down Cope Hall Lane pursued by Horse and a fierce hand-to-hand struggle took place between

Sometimes called Skinner's Green Lane and sometimes Cope Hall Lane, the road that crosses Round Hill was the site of desperate fighting as the Royalist Horse tried to cut down retreating Londoners, but themselves fell prey to musketeers firing from behind the hedges.

the banked hedgerows on either side. Only point-blank musketry from the fields to the north halted the Royalists' pursuit, allowing the Trained Bands to regroup on the hillside.

As the Londoners settled in to their new position two regiments of Royalist Foot, presumably from Gerard's Tertio, attacked them, probably thinking that as they had already fallen back once they would be easier to break, but they weren't. The attack of the Royalist infantry on the common lacked the determination and élan expected of the redoubtable royal Horse, and several accounts accuse them of refusing to advance into the storm of shot. Two more regiments of Horse, this time from the Londoners' right flank, and probably belonging to Colonel Charles Gerard's Brigade of Horse, fiercely charged and actually managed to surround the Londoners; at one stage they even got across the lane and among the battery, dragging away one light piece. There is some evidence to suggest that this may have been the occasion when the Royalists adopted the Parliamentarian field sign of a sprig of greenery jammed into their helmets or hat bands, although this is frequently attributed to an incident towards the end of the fight in the north. Forced into an untidy stand or square, the musketeers must have knelt beneath the protecting shafts of the pikemen and fired as fast as they could at point-blank range into the seething mass of horsemen, who, in turn, unable to force their mounts forward against the 'stabbing wall of brite steele', fired their pistols 'in their teeth'. Whoever was commanding this sector of the Royalist line, possibly Colonel Gilbert Gerard, knew exactly what he was doing because when the Horse were beaten off but before the Londoners had time to re-form, he sent in another infantry attack. This time it was successful and the whole block of Parliamentarian infantry recoiled. Yet still their morale held. They rallied and advanced, retaking their ground. There is some indication that they might have been assisted by cavalry as the Royalist Gwyn records that the arrival of Horse made his regiment, Lloyd's, retire into a field, although Gwyn himself, clutching the colours, was obliged to leap a hedge and a ditch to do so. At one point the Trained Bands fired another point-blank volley into the charging Royalist Horse and knocked down so many that the ground was strewn with 'men and horses rolling on the heath'.

The southern slope of Round Hill facing east. The London regiments retired to this slope to get away from the guns on the open land near the modern water-tower. However, do bear in mind there is a well-argued case for a totally different location!

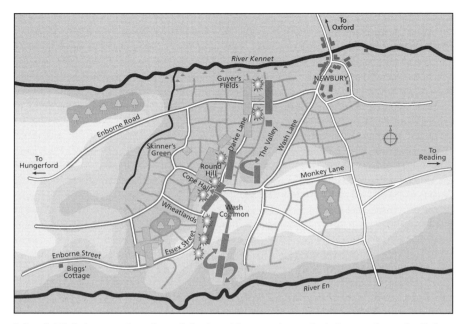

Map 9: Fighting continued until dusk, with several attacks being made as the light failed. Rupert's Horse meanwhile probed the southern extremities.

The unknown Royalist officer whose letter is in the Rupert Correspondence relates in detail his role in the attack across the common and down the lane and describes just how bitter the fighting was. Finally the Royalists conceded that they could not take the hill and after three hours of continuous fighting the Red and Blue Regiments of untested militia Foot could rest; Foster states they 'stood like so many stakes against the shot of the cannons, quitting themselves like men of undaunted spirit'. It had cost them dearly but in one of the most amazing actions of the battle, if not the whole war, they had held their own against several determined combined arms attacks and prevented a breakthrough in the centre.

Grinding Stalemate

Throughout these trials inflicted upon the two London regiments, assaults were repeatedly made against Essex's men. Sir John Byron's criticism of the efforts of the Foot in the southern sector seems exceptionally harsh and unfair, for they were involved for several hours with attacks across Enborne Street on the three brigades dug in behind the common hedge. All along this high ground the regiments of Colonel John Belasyse and those elements of Colonel Sir Gilbert Gerard's Tertio that were not trying to break the Londoners were in action against Essex's, Holbourne's and Barclay's Brigades of Foot, and the battle raged, ebbed and flowed until finally the light failed. It is reputed that Essex's horse dropped dead from exhaustion.

It was getting towards the end of the day. In the north Robartes and Vavasour continued their firefight; one unidentified Royalist officer was ordered to reconnoitre the situation with a view to ensuring they were not about to be outflanked and turned, but he found the area secured – at stalemate. In the centre Skippon, though driven back and forced to commit more troops than he would have wished, had held the Round Hill and kept the vital lanes. He had called in the Reserve, all but the Orange Regiment of the City of London Auxiliaries, from Skinner's Green to the centre opposite Monkey Lane and he had brought his guns up the steep slope. Byron retained his foothold in the central enclosures and could not be budged. In the south Rupert's cavalry licked their wounds, taking consolation from having once again beaten their counterparts and driven them from their ground. The main Parliamentarian attacking force, Essex's Wing, had failed to break through to the London road but his Horse, despite their mauling, had rallied and drawn up yet again behind the Foot manning the improvised field-barricades on the edge of Wash Common. All along the line exhaustion set in. The first battle of Newbury had come to a stuttering halt.

Afterwards

As night fell both sides drew apart, although sporadic shooting and skirmishing took place well into the night – 'the glimmer of matches and the flashing of the firearms served to show each other where the other lay' – but by midnight they had totally disengaged. Clashes must have happened all over the area, including down by the En where skeletons, supposedly from the battle, were discovered when the mill race was dammed. The Royalist 'ruse de guerre' of launching an attack wearing the Parliamentarian field sign is also tied to this part of the battle, and linked to an attempt on Essex's baggage, although other Royalist accounts indicate they were preoccupied in withdrawing from the field, getting over the Kennet and seeking quarters in Speen and the surrounding villages. The Army Councils of both sides seem to have met and discussed the state of their armies, the number of casualties (reports vary, but the figure was about 1,200 on each side), and their options for the next day.

Essex's plan was still feasible and the Parliamentarian soldiers seem to have expected the battle to continue. Loath to give up the ground they held, they virtually camped where they stood, making the best use of whatever cover they could find and erecting make-do shelters. Despite post-battle fatigue, a lack of provisions and a miserable rain-soaked night, their morale was strangely high; they had been held but not beaten, and the inexperienced units had done well; even their Horse, which had been driven off by the superior Royalist cavalry, had rallied and readied themselves to fight again. They were determined that the next day they would 'force our way through them or dye', but it was a determination fostered by lack of food and their desperate strategic position – it was long way back to Gloucester and a retreat to Southampton would leave them dangerously exposed. The Royalist soldiers must have been exceptionally tired, having made a forced march and then fought all day, and were doubtless demoralised, having failed to drive their opponents from the field. It can be supposed that they left pickets and grand guards to keep watch and secure their ground too, but much of the army apparently fell back to its camp at the bottom end of Wash Lane and into Newbury itself. Byron called surrendering such hard-fought ground 'foolish' and 'knavish', and called the Foot 'jades'. Intelligence reports said they were in 'a great fright' and accused them of 'stealing away from their arms in the night'.

The royal high command now faced another problem: lack of gunpowder. They had used 80 of their 90 barrels of it, which they reckoned was three times as much as they had expended at Edgehill. At that rate of consumption they could sustain only another one hour's fighting. In addition there was also a growing concern about supplies of matchcord and shot for the guns. During the early evening they had sent to Oxford for more, the order arriving between 7.00 and 8.00pm. By 3.00am Sir John Heydon, Lieutenant-General of the Ordnance, had sent off 50 barrels plus more ammunition and match, in a train of thirteen wagons, but it was too late. By the time the train reached Newbury, affairs had taken a dramatic turn.

At daybreak Essex again roused and arrayed his men in battle formation and let his guns open up to announce that they were ready to offer battle for the second day. Rupert was all for barring the Parliamentarians' way with whatever force they could muster, but he was out-voted in Council, which argued that the ground was as unfavourable as it had been the day before when they could make little headway. The accepted story is that without sufficient powder the Royalists could not accept the challenge and so must have warily watched as the Parliamentarians advanced, regretting they had not the stuff of war to fight them. Essex gave orders to local parishes to bury the many dead; Foster noted seeing about a hundred corpses that had been stripped by looters. His own wounded men were loaded on to his wagons and, after brushing the Royalist pickets aside, marched over Wash Common for his base in London. We do not know which route they took. Monkey Lane seems perilously close to the royal lines, but they certainly crossed the Common, halting several times and seeming to deploy for a fight in order to ascertain the Royalists' true intentions, before continuing along the south side of the Kennet heading for the garrisoned depot at Reading.

That the King did not order an attack is often ascribed to the lack of powder but he may have been influenced by the losses incurred, especially by his 'best troops', and among his nobility and personal friends. Bulstrode compared the losses as staking 'pearls against pebbles'. The general exhaustion of his army after a long forced march and the trauma of battle should also be considered. It has been argued that Essex should have attacked and forced another battle but this does not seem to have entered his thinking as he maintained his campaign objective and fell back to his base. Both belong to the 'what if' view of history, but one can only imagine the casualties that would have been sustained if the King had fallen back into Newbury and Essex had assaulted the fortified town. Judging commanders out of their time and with hindsight is not a rewarding pastime.

What is not in any doubt, however, is that Rupert was not one for giving up and letting his enemy go. Though his uncle and his staff seem to have accepted the idea that Essex's army could slip past them and away, Rupert organised a pursuit, taking much of his Horse with him, as well as Lisle's commanded muskets. Shortly before 4.00pm, in a narrow hedged lane near Aldermaston, possibly near Brimpton, they attacked the tail of the Parliamentarian column. Essex had given command of the rear to Colonel John Middleton, who had half his brigade of Horse with him, as well as his own, Meldrum's and Sheffield's regiments supported by Colonel Henry Barclay and 600 commanded musketeers. The incident is recorded by Sergeant Foster of the Red Regiment, which had the rear of the Main Battle (which also supports the view that they were not part of Essex's vanguard). He accuses the Horse of not daring to stand against the Royalists and fleeing before contact, crashing into and riding down their own Foot and causing panic in the column. Wagons were overturned and some abandoned as drivers cut the traces and rode off on the teams. Rupert's men 'came on very fiercely, having their foot on the other side of the hedges', but Foster tells us they were met by regiments of the London Brigade which deployed among the hedges and fired at them, and unlimbered and fired ten or twelve light guns at them. The impetus of the attack overran the guns and drove the Londoners back, but they rallied, formed a secure defence and volleyed again and again. They stemmed the rout, stopped the Royalists' advance, 'slew many of them' and took prisoners. The incident ended spectacularly at about 5.00pm when a powder wagon, having spilt its load when it was rolled over in the panic, suddenly ignited. The explosion killed two men, badly burnt seven others and injured scores more. In the resulting confusion the Royalists tried to take away two of the guns they had overrun but again the Londoners pushed forward and prevented it. Rupert's men withdrew, and one account implies that they left 'many colours of the King's cornets' behind them.

Essex took stock of the situation and patched up the disaster as best he could, but pressed on in his march. His army crossed the Kennet at Padworth and then marched into Theale at about 10.00pm that night. The next morning, Friday 22 September, they continued to Reading, where they were welcomed with great rejoicing. By 26 September Essex himself was in London for a grand review of the London regiments who had marched with him. His reception was ecstatic. By the 28th his army had retired to Windsor and Essex once again was fêted by the capital's crowds as the London Brigade, very much the heroes of the hour, joyfully entered the city in triumph, having relieved Gloucester, stormed Cirencester, fought the King to a standstill at Newbury and finally come safe home.

The King wisely consolidated his position by putting a strong garrison of 200 infantry from Earl Rivers' Regiment, 25 cavalry and 4 guns under Lieutenant-Colonel John Boys into Donnington Castle. This dominating structure was subsequently improved with earthworks and became a troublesome thorn in Parliament's side, as well as forming part of the 'ring of bright steel' around Oxford. However, it was not such a joyful royal army that marched north from Donnington to Oxford. They had buried the dead, and tended to their fallen senior officers, including Falkland, Caernarvon and Lord Sunderland, who had been killed by roundshot while serving as a trooper in the Lifeguard. They were laid in state in the Newbury Guildhall (demolished 1827).

The royal Council of War had never been a harmonious body, not even in victory, and now, having failed to win the battle and lost many friends, they fell to quarrelling even more. Anger and jealousy were rife and accusations of cowardice, lack of planning and lack of commitment flew everywhere. The mood in Oxford, according to Clarendon, was one of 'dejection of mind, discontent and secret mutiny'. They knew they had won the strategic victory, but somehow they had thrown it all away in a battle they did not think they had to fight. What was more, Lord Falkland's 'great voice of reason' and his arbitration and political skills were much missed.

Conclusion

Newbury I was not a classic battle fought in drill-book formations in open fields. The nature of the terrain made it more of a bitter struggle often in confined spaces and at close quarters. Men fought on foot and on horseback for control of narrow lanes and gaps in hedgerows and, for a lot of the action, had to endure short-range artillery fire. Without an overall plan the Royalist brigade commanders did the best they could in the situations in which they found themselves, and often their strenuous efforts resulted in their Parliamentarian counterparts being switched from one sector to another or brought up from the Reserve to be flung into gaps to prevent disaster. Finding a time format to understand the battle in a sequential framework is difficult for it appears a piecemeal affair both geographically and chronologically, and we cannot be certain of what was happening where at particular times. There are also major disagreements about the story of the battle in the primary sources. However, despite all the gaps in our knowledge, we can say that it was a hard-fought battle and that both sides displayed great heroism and soldierly expertise.

Tactically Parliament had won. Essex's plan to get round the south side of Newbury with all his army worked because the basic strategic topographical consideration remained the same all day. In the morning he took the lanes up to the high ground and Round Hill itself, which dominated the common, thus both facilitating and preventing serious opposition to his intended move to Reading. During the day Skippon maintained this objective, gradually moving units and vehicles to the hill or south of it. By the end of the day Parliament still held the hill and the Royalists' lack of powder meant they could not take it. Although the Royalists could claim they still blocked the way and Essex had not forced a path through to Reading, the morale of both the soldiers and the high command seems to have evaporated. Their army had quit the field, handing the victory to Essex. The Royalist campaign aim was frustrated, for to continue would have been to sustain unacceptable losses and there was no militarily sensible option other than to retire.

Strategically both sides had been losers. The King had failed to take Gloucester and failed to prevent Essex returning to London, whereas Essex might have relieved Gloucester but he had failed to grasp the opportunity to destroy the King's army.

Chapter Five

THE SECOND BATTLE OF NEWBURY

By the end of October 1644 the fortunes of war, which had turned at Newbury I, had swung more in favour of the Parliamentarian cause. Marston Moor had been a crushing defeat for the Royalists and their erstwhile hero Prince Rupert found himself ostracised from the military circles that once lauded his successes. New stars, too, were rising for Parliament in the form of Sir Thomas Fairfax and the promising cavalry commander Oliver Cromwell.

The Campaign

However, against this run of events, on 2 September 1644 at Lostwithiel in Cornwall King Charles I's Army of Oxford had successfully defeated Parliament's Lord-General, Robert Devereux, Earl of Essex, forcing him to flee in a fishing boat. His army surrendered but was allowed to go free. Having relinquished their guns, muskets, pikes and equipment, the men marched out of Lostwithiel, then, contrary to the rules of war, many of them were attacked and plundered of food, shoes and almost everything else; some were even killed. Their return has been called a 'death march'. Without leaders or weapons, half-starved and demoralised, Essex's army had been knocked out of the war and the West Country came under Royalist control. In addition to this setback, Parliament's other main force, Sir William Waller's Army of the Southern Association, had not fully recovered from Roundway Down and had also met with a reverse at Cropredy. The units had been severely cut up and many of them had fed detachments into garrisons. Overall, things did not look good for Parliament.

Seeking to take advantage of this favourable situation, made even more attractive by the dispersed nature of Waller's men, the King and his Council planned a series of moves to advance out of the west. The plan was to rid the region south of the King's base at Oxford of Parliamentarian troops and then proceed into quarters, which they hoped might be found in East Anglia. The initial stage entailed a demonstrative march in strength through the south-west and the raising of the on-going sieges of Basing House near Basingstoke, Donnington Castle near Newbury and Banbury. These belea-guered garrisons had been temporarily isolated while the King's army had been campaigning in Devon and Cornwall. The Royalists' first target was the relief of Basing, and they began a steady if slow march eastward from Exeter bound for central southern England.

As the army marched through Somerset, Charles was joined by his nephew Prince Rupert at South Perrot on 30 September. The King was not pleased by the meeting; Rupert reported the details of his defeat at Marston Moor, and blame and recriminations were rife. The Royalist plans now appear to have been revised and a strike at the scattered Parliamentarian forces was brought into the scheme. However, rather than join the army and command the Horse for the whole enterprise, as was expected, the Prince was sent with a significant body of troops to take control of Bristol, in the hope that his presence there would attract attention and divert part of Waller's army to keep watch on him. The King, intent upon the relief of the three garrisons and attacking his dispersed foe, made for Blandford and then Salisbury, entering the city on or around 15 October.

Meanwhile, Waller's men were not totally dispirited by their recent defeats. Recruiting began, and Waller seems to have been able to field a substantial brigade of Horse. Essex reassembled his army at Portsmouth, where he surprisingly quickly re-equipped and re-enthused his men, although he had lost many to desertion. To increase his strength, Parliament ordered Edward Montagu, Earl of Manchester, and his Army of the Eastern Association, which had been part of the victorious forces at Marston Moor, to join with him and form a tripartite command. It was a sound military plan but there were tensions between the three Parliamentarian commanders. Waller had blamed Essex for his defeat at Roundway Down, and Essex saw

---

WALLER'S ARMY
The battles at Cheriton and Cropredy had all taken their toll on Waller's army as it struggled to recover from the disaster of Roundway Down. It was in a poor state and needed time to recuperate and rebuild. The Calendar of State Papers Domestic lists many of Waller's Foot being trans-ferred to garrisons in the south-west so that by the time of Newbury II the only references are to his Horse. Several secondary sources say Waller's infantry fought at Newbury II under Major-General Holborne, and some place them with Waller's night march. I remain to be convinced of either, although new evidence may prove them to have been present.

Manchester as a rival for supreme command. Manchester had also fallen out with his Lieutenant-General of Horse, the up-and-coming Oliver Cromwell. Despite their differences, an uneasy Council of War responded quickly to the growing Royalist threat. While Essex continued his build-up in Portsmouth, Waller gathered his scattered cavalry army around Sherborne, and then, when the King's army arrived in the area, fell back to Andover. Meanwhile Manchester rallied his regiments at Reading before interpreting his orders to march into the west to join Adjutant-General Horton's siege of Donnington. Intentionally or not, the Parliamentarian forces were concentrating. Meanwhile the King's plans began to fail as Waller ignored Rupert's move to Bristol, and thus the move served only to reduce the King's own numbers and weaken the royal army.

The Royalist Council agreed to strike at Waller's relatively small force in Andover and on 18 October advanced against him. The Parliamentarian general, heavily outnumbered and without Foot to hold ground, refused to fight and fell back towards Basingstoke, but not before George, Lord Goring had engaged his forces with 200 Royalist troopers and inflicted a stinging

---

ESSEX'S ARMY

After the disaster of the Cornish campaign the remnants of Essex's army that had struggled into Southampton and Portsmouth had to be reclothed, re-equipped and reorganised. Full details of this feat can be found in S. Peachy and A. Turton's *Old Robin's Foot* (Partizan Press, 1987), but it is worth noting here that despite the heroic efforts, his army was never the same. It was considerably reduced and one of the London brigades was broken up. The Yellow Regiment of the City of London Auxiliaries which Essex had left to garrison Weymouth was transferred to Robartes' command in Plymouth, and the pitiful remains of Colonel Whichcot's Green Regiment and Colonel Gower's Orange Regiment of the City of London Auxiliaries were paid off and marched back to London. The Plymouth regiments, including Colonel Carre's Foot and Colonel Layton's Horse, were sent by sea back to their homes, but there seem to have been only about 200 of them left. Of the 150 officers and men remaining in Colonel John Weare's Regiment of Foot, 36 were absorbed into Essex's own regiment, and the rest presumably took ship for home as well. Essex optimistically ordered 6,000 muskets, 1,000 pikes and 260 officers' polearms plus 80 drums for his new infantry but it would seem he only had some 3,000 men all ranks when they mustered for the first time at Southwick House near Portchester. These men he led to Newbury II.

blow, taking a number of prisoners including Colonel Carre and Captain Scott, who died of his wounds. A party of Horse was also dispatched to Donnington Castle, where Horton's and Manchester's besieging force, which had been unwilling to attempt a storm, abandoned their efforts on the 18th or 19th in the face of an advancing army and retired, allowing the Royalists uncontested access. Horton fell back to Abingdon and Manchester towards Reading. The King was now joined by his Lord-

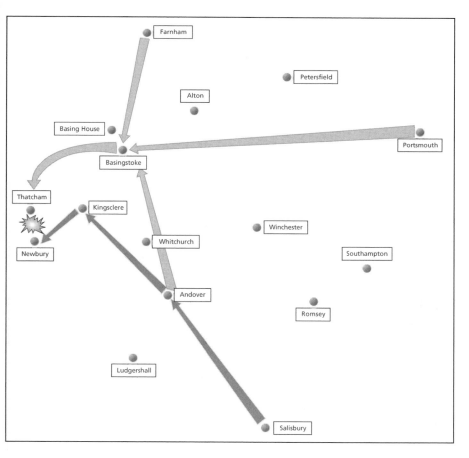

Map 10: The King tried to reach Basing House but was thwarted by the Parliamentarian rendezvous at Basingstoke. He withdrew to Newbury but was shadowed and threatened by the united armies of Essex, Manchester and Waller.

General, Patrick Ruthven, now Earl of Brentford, and by Thomas Wentworth, Earl of Cleveland and their respective forces, which had been sent to relieve Portland. The Royalist march continued.

Essex, too, was massing his forces and called a General Rendezvous of the Three Armies at Basingstoke on 20 October. Manchester was slow to bring in all his regiments, but did get several there so that the numbers present at the rendezvous caused the Royalists to halt at Kingsclere, where the King became wary about the intended relief of Basing. Royalist spies had reported that the enemy was superior in cavalry and that the Basingstoke countryside was more open than it was around Newbury and thus better suited to that arm. His doubts were exacerbated when Captain Fincher of Waller's army led a strong enemy cavalry probe around Kingsclere. Although the Parliamentarians were soon seen off, the whole incident left the King anxious. The Marquis of Winchester's garrison in Basing House was thus temporarily abandoned to its fate as the royal army swung northwards for Newbury, which they reached quickly and easily, camping for the night on Red Heath, south-west of Wash Common, while the King and his staff entered the town.

Over the next few days the royal army rested in and around the busy Berkshire town. The garrison at Donnington Castle was relieved, and for the second time in the war Newbury was occupied by a large royal army. The

MANCHESTER'S ARMY

Manchester had not wanted to join with Essex and Waller but his request to his political masters to allow him to remain in the area of St Albans was denied. A contemporary siege document tells us that he had eight of his nine regiments at Donnington, which supposes one had yet to join the field army and was probably still in Reading; it is likely that it came up with the London Brigade. Both Manchester's Foot and Horse were considerably numerically superior to those in either Essex's or Waller's armies. A typical Eastern Association Foot regiment, Pickering's, mustered nearly 600 men in July 1644 while most regiments with Essex had between 200 and 300. Muster returns and estimates suggest Essex's and Waller's regiments of Horse were even smaller by comparison. No records exist of how Manchester and Crawford organised the brigades for Newbury II, but there is very little to suggest they changed much from Marston Moor and they most likely brought together the three Foot regiments that had missed that action. Manchester was estimated to have had 3,000 Foot and 1,800 Horse and dragoons with him on Clay Hill, in addition to the London Brigade.

garrison commander of Donnington was John Boys, Lieutenant-Colonel of Earl Rivers' Regiment of Foot, who had a brother fighting in Manchester's army. Boys had done prodigious work with only 250 Foot, 25 Horse and 4 guns and was knighted for his services and promoted to colonel. However, the King now compounded his Rupert-and-Bristol error by dispatching another of his most competent senior officers, James Compton, Earl of Northampton, with three regiments of Horse, Gwyn says 1,500 men, which the King could ill-afford to lose. Compton was to investigate the situation and if possible relieve Banbury, which was being held by one of his younger brothers, Sir William Compton.

Donnington Castle had been garrisoned by the Royalists since Newbury I. Boys had dug a large star fort earthwork around the castle and proved very

The dramatic remains of the gatehouse at Donnington Castle.

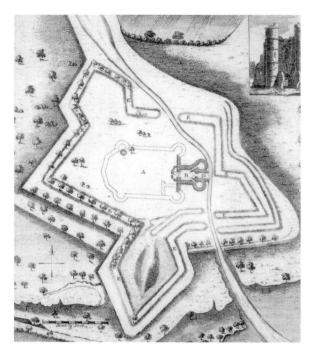

A plan of the fortifications which surrounded Donnington Castle. Note the dominant south bastion that overlooked the Oxford road bridge to the south-east.

effective at controlling the area and subduing the pro-Parliament town. He had also withstood both a determined assault by a force of 3,000 men led by Middleton, and a prolonged siege, although a twelve-day bombardment by Horton's guns and a further nineteen days' bombardment from Manchester's had brought down many of the medieval walls and pounded much of the masonry to rubble. Only the gatehouse towers remain today.

As the Royalists had marched north to Newbury, they had been shadowed by Parliamentarian cavalry and skirmishing ensued as the generals of the combined armies sought a way to cut the King's line of communication by getting between him and Oxford. Instead of offering him battle or attacking him on the march, the Parliamentarians manoeuvred east of Newbury so as to both threaten the King's route to Oxford and also prevent the Royalists getting between them and London. Such a move also enabled them to protect their depots at Reading and Windsor. Reluctant to have to cross the River Kennet under fire, the Parliamentarian commanders hoped to advance upon the King's army on the north bank of the river. Thus they marched north-east from Basingstoke, up the Reading Road, and then swung westward for Newbury. The infantry marched via Swallowfield and the cavalry via Aldermaston, with mounted patrols clashing around Thatcham as both sides sent out reconnaissance parties to seek intelligence, and prepared for an engagement. The Parliamentarians tried to 'beat up' various Royalist cavalry quarters. According to the *Mercurius Aulicus,* one such attack was repulsed by the reformado Lieutenant-General Bovel (or Bovill), who then was serving as the Lieutenant-Colonel of Sir Francis Doddington's Regiment. The Royalists dug entrenchments and mounted their batteries, while the Parliamentarians sought to bring all their diverse contingents together. Some units from Manchester's Eastern Association were marching down from Reading while those which had been at Basingstoke marched to meet them, crossing the Kennet at Lodge Farm, a ford near Padworth. Despite a skirmish with a very strong Royalist outpost, they all marched to and took Bucklebury Common, where they began laying out a large encampment. Local tradition says another cavalry action took place west of Thatcham in Dunston Park and Red Field, and that those killed here were buried near Mortimer Farm, although this needs archaeological investigation. Waller established his headquarters at Thatcham and so, with Henwick also taken, the line of march to Reading was secure. If the King had hoped his men might spend the winter in Newbury, with the weather forcing the Parliamentarians to retire, he was to be disappointed, because, as at Newbury I, the two armies had come too close to each other for either to march away with impunity. To add to Parliament's problems, the ground was complicated with rolling hills, rivers, villages and hedges. Again this was not to be the type of open battlefield that most armies of the period sought.

Meanwhile Essex marched up with the rest of his army and Waller's, and they settled at Bradfield and on Beenham Heath, although the Earl himself was now very ill, possibly suffering from exposure, exhaustion and a severe chill. His unstinting exertions during the Lostwithiel campaign, the rebuilding of his army and the ceaseless marches in the wet finally took their toll and forced him to return to Reading in a mattress-padded coach. His absence was concealed from the troops. On Friday 25 October a general rendezvous was staged on Bucklebury heath, and despite Symonds' comment 'Noe action all this day', a raid was made upon the Royalist Horse quarters in Shaw and a small body of Parliamentarians managed to get up on to Clay Hill, then called High Dike, north-east of Newbury. Both parties were driven off by Royalist troops under Prince Maurice, including Foot and dragoons from his own regiments. However, a larger Parliamentarian detachment gained possession of the hill again on the 26th, in the process managing to overrun a battery of four guns with a grand guard of 400 Foot. This high ground overlooked the Oxford road, so the Parliamentarians quickly hauled more guns on to the crest. A short artillery duel followed but

Manchester's position on Clay Hill, with the arrows indicating the direction of his major attack across Long Lane in the foreground.

achieved very little, although Ludlow's Wiltshire Horse on the lower slopes of Clay Hill suffered casualties, including Ludlow's cousin Gabriel, who had his belly torn open and his hip smashed. Musket exchanges began in the evening and Symonds records that sporadic shooting went on all night. However, the Parliamentarian forces had achieved their objective of severing the King's communications with his Oxford base.

The King had now several strategic options. First, he was pressed to attack the hill immediately and, while the gunners were distracted, march his army north and return to Oxford. Secondly, he was urged to fall back into the west, where he could be reinforced and then seek a more advantageous battlefield. Thirdly, he was advised to strike south, relieving Basing and burning pro-Parliament Basingstoke. Fourthly, some argued for him to launch an all-out attack on the Parliamentarians gathering to the east. The trouble with marching away in any direction was that the armies were too close: any sort of withdrawal would present the other side with an excellent opportunity to fall upon the retreating army's flank or rear and partially destroy it. Going to Oxford was also out of the question, for if the royal army retreated to its safety it would have achieved nothing since Lostwithiel and would have let slip a golden opportunity to add the south to its recent triumphs in the west. North Newbury was not a bad position, and probably far better than any vague venue in the west, so Charles decided to hold his ground and fight, to which end he would recall both Rupert from Bristol and Northampton from Banbury. He needed all the men he could get, and he

needed them at Newbury, where, rather than attack, he was obliged to opt for a fifth option, taking up a defensive position north of the town.

The Plans

The Royalists were outnumbered and lacked good intelligence. The King actually berated the people of the town as 'wicked Roundheads' as they brought him little or no information on the movements of his enemies, and the Parliamentarian press claimed he issued instructions to burn the town rather than let it fall into enemy hands. However, the Royalists had four major strongpoints: Prince Maurice held the village of Speen in the west, Sir John Boys was reinforced in Donnington Castle in the north, and Lord Astley manned both Mr Doleman's House (now Shaw House) and the neighbouring Shaw village in the east. All four positions had been fortified with earthworks and improvised barricades. Between Clay Hill and Newbury lay the River Lambourne, which ran through Donnington and Shaw across the Royalists' front in a north-easterly direction and flowed into the Kennet east of Newbury. Both Donnington Castle and Shaw House, built by the clothier Sir Thomas Doleman (hence some confusion about its name in the sources), lay on the Lambourne's north bank, which occasioned some Royalist forces, especially those of Astley's command, to be deployed with their backs to the water.

It was not a formidable river but it was still an obstacle. Like most rivers

The River Lambourne; although not very deep, it was a substantial obstacle to movement.

in the area, it was some 2m to 4m wide, about 1m to 2m deep, had a deep mud bottom and was usually quite full. Guns could not traverse it, although other troops could wade across with difficulty. It provided a significant impediment to movement, halting charges from both Foot and Horse. Several sources say both the Lambourne and the Kennet were in flood at the time of the battle, which would have meant their floodplains were water-logged so that virtually all troop movement through them was impossible. Added to this, the areas between most of these strongpoints were full of enclosures, most with thick surrounding hedges that also impeded attacks and gave cover to the defenders. The Royalists, though, had the advantage of the more open field systems in Speenhamland so they could redeploy more easily when necessary.

The King's army held a strong defensive position, the fortified works making it ominously difficult to attack. This was not lost on Waller and Manchester, upon whom the divided command had settled since Essex's worsening condition prevented him from returning to the campaign.

However, from their vantage point on Clay Hill the two commanders surveyed the triangle of strongpoints and pondered their options. One option they did not have was to do nothing. They had gained the strategic advantage, and if they engaged immediately the odds would be greatly in their favour, as Rupert and Northampton had not yet arrived with their experienced Horse. Moreover, a major victory at Newbury could destroy the King's army and bring the war to a rapid close. They had to attack.

Waller and Manchester decided that a frontal attack from east to west with the strongly fortified Shaw House in the centre would be both risky and costly, especially as they had to cross the Lambourne and the guns of Donnington Castle could support the Royalists' left flank. Such an attack would also channel their larger army into a narrow front and thus negate their superior numbers. They needed a plan that would not only divide the Royalists' firepower but also stretch their defensive capabilities. It was decided to try a rear attack. They would divide their forces. Manchester, with 3,000 of his own Foot, supported by 1,500 Horse in three brigades, one each from Waller's army, the Eastern Association and the London Horse, would keep the Royalists facing Clay Hill busy, while Waller, with the rest

The view from Clay Hill across to Shaw; this is the ground over which Manchester launched his final attack.

of his cavalry, all of Essex's army, Harrington's London Brigade and Cromwell leading the remainder of the Eastern Association Horse, would undertake a long march, stealthily circumnavigating the whole Royalist position and eventually coming out on the other side of Newbury to attack Speen from the west, effectively taking the King's army in the rear.

Edward Walker noted, however, that this possibility had been foreseen: Prince Maurice's men in Speen had already begun deploying their guns and digging impromptu works facing west. Elsewhere, too, they dug works and 'fortify'd the Avenues'. Regrettably we have even less contemporary information about the battle plan and the deployment of the royal army than we do for Newbury I, and what we have is tricky to untangle and at times contradictory. However, we can glean certain facts from the accounts: we know, for example, that the recently ennobled Jacob, Lord Astley, hero of Edgehill and Lieutenant-General of the Foot, had command of the right wing facing east; Prince Maurice of the Palatinate with his Western Army was in command of the left wing facing west; and the King himself took command of the centre facing north. It was an all-round, semi-circular defence with its base resting on the Kennet, with Newbury at its centre.

In the east Astley had two brigades of Foot under his command: Colonel George Lisle had the left, north of the Lambourne, while Sir Bernard Astley had the right, south of the Lambourne and rather distant from Shaw. This might be rather too simplistic a divide, as some of Sir Bernard's men were in the buildings of Shaw village on the north bank, but it serves to help understand events.

Lisle's command stretched from Shaw village on his right northwards along Long Lane (Shaw Road) to some enclosures on his left, with Shaw House, its outbuildings and gardens serving as a bastion at its rear centre. Lisle spread his tertio along this line, using the hedgerows and lanes as defensive features. He put several regiments into the Shaw House complex, placing them under Lieutenant-Colonel Richard Page, who Symonds says had 1,000 muskets in the buildings. In the fields behind the house was Lisle's reserve, including the Prince of Wales's Regiment of Horse and some dragoons. Lisle seems also to have formed a line along the bridleway to Curridge on the east slopes of Brick-kiln Hill, but he was doubtless reluctant to extend his left too far into the open fields hereabouts. There is a significant descent in the bridleway before Highwood Farm, which may represent the furthest point of Lisle's left as it can be covered by the higher ground to its rear.

Colonel Sir Bernard Astley's Tertio, which was probably weaker than some others in the army, had the job of sealing the gap between Shaw and Newbury, which meant linking up with the left of Lisle's Tertio at Shaw village and resting his right flank on Newbury Marsh. Astley made good use of the area's buildings, including those in Shaw village, a large house in Shaw Park and those in north Newbury's Speenhamland hamlet, notably a fortified mill on the Kennet. His main line, however, was set back and ran southwards, at a distance west of but roughly parallel to the line of the modern road. This area offered natural defensive advantages, and each field hedge and garden was lined with parties of musketeers, while to their front the gaps between houses and in hedges were sealed with barricades. Astley was perhaps held back because a lot of the ground to his front was flooded and thus an attack across it seemed unlikely; by not allocating all his troops to a defensive front line, they would be in a better position to send support elsewhere if required.

Across the centre of the field, and facing any attack along the Oxford road, a great breastwork was thrown up behind which the majority of the Royalist heavy artillery was deployed. Behind the guns stood the Horse, placed in the open fields around Speenhamland to support and defend the guns but also able to move left or right to add their weight to any developing situation. Sir Humphrey Bennet's Brigade of Horse was drawn up to the left

The remains of the curtain wall of Donnington Castle which provided ample breastwork cover for the Royalist defenders.

rear of this main body of cavalry, between Newbury and Speen, to counter any breakthrough by the Parliamentarian Horse through the riverside enclosures south of Speen church. The King ordered Colonel Thomas Blagge's Tertio to form the core of the Reserve and hold this central position, as well as putting a force into Donnington village. In Donnington Castle itself Sir John Boys and what was now, or was shortly to become, his regiment of Foot and his troop of Horse manned their guns, the gatehouse, the rubble walls and the earthworks.

All over the field men dug fortifications. Near the Kennet a breastwork covered the Great West Road, and around Shaw House the Royalists apparently converted some supposedly ancient earthworks, although they seem more like Elizabethan gardening features. We are told that every mound around Shaw had a trench, ditch and log work ensconced upon it, while a short terrace of cottages known as 'Hop Gardens' east of the old Rectory was boarded up and loopholed. In the centre was the Oxford road breastwork, while in the west on Speen Hill it is presumed a series of trenches had been dug and palisaded, including major traverses, and a large redoubt was even begun at the entrance to Wickham Heath between two hedges, although

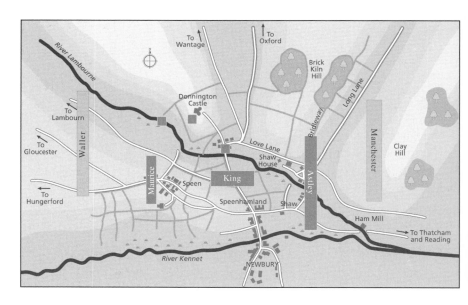

Map 11: The Royalists deployed in a defensive semi-circle north of the Kennet, making use of buildings as strongpoints and rivers as barriers to flanking moves. This obliged Manchester and Waller to devise a daring two-pronged attack.

how much of this is 'embroidered' we cannot tell. There was certainly a large defensive barricade with cross ditches dug deeper and guns set in the gaps, but any potential archaeological study has been thwarted by the creation of the Newbury bypass, which was cut through its likely position.

A Victorian account has the King's Lifeguard from Blagge's Tertio accompanying his majesty to Bagner but it is now thought that this was a strong vedette rather than a whole regiment of guards led by the monarch. On the left, with his front line of guns on a rise crossed by the Great West Road, Maurice had his tertio of Western Foot and his small brigade of Western Horse, plus the Duke of York's Regiment of Foot in support. Maurice also commanded Sir John Douglas's grand guard of 200 Foot and 300 Horse, which was supposedly thrown out to the village of Boxford north-west of Speen to watch for any encircling move and defend a crossing of the Lambourne. The Victorian writer Ditchfield tells us that 'the Royal Standard waved upon Speen Moor' – but this would have put the King west of Speen and thus outside his own defensive ring.

This formidable defensive ring of villages – Speen, Bagner, Donnington, Shaw and the Speenhamland suburb of north Newbury, plus the complexes of Donnington Castle and Shaw House – was strongly held and well fortified. In addition, the Lambourne River ran across much of the front and works had been thrown up in the open fields, while intervening hedges were banked and ditched; the Rocque map shows that both ends of this inverted semi-circle rested upon ground described as marsh. The Parliamentarians occupied Clay Hill and the high ground extending to Ashmore Green and Cold Ash. Didsbury makes the point that the situation more closely resembled the prelude to a siege than the deployment for a field engagement.

Waller and the West

Waller began his 13-mile march late in the evening (one source says about midnight) on 26 October, taking what appears to be a rather strange route until we look at Rocque's map of 1752/3. Moving by the major roads of the day, he marched from his headquarters in Thatcham via the deployment assembly area behind Clay Hill northwards via Cold Ash to the village of Hermitage. Next his force went west to Prior's Court, then through Chievely to North Heath, where the men stopped for a few hours' rest. They did, however, intercept several Royalist provision wagons which they despoiled, and rounded up about a hundred stragglers and late-comers, whom they made prisoner. News also reached them of the successful storm of Newcastle, which must have boosted their morale. They then went south to

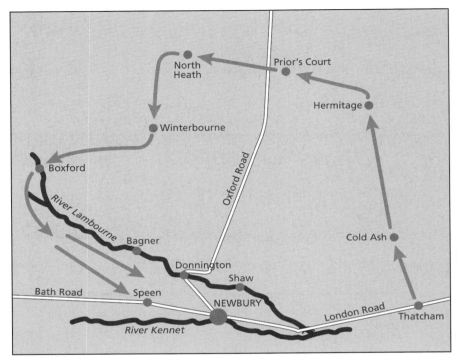

Map 12: Waller's long night march hooked around the north of Newbury and brought his army to the west of the town.

Winterbourn and swung south-west for Boxford and the bridge across the Lambourne River. Sir John Boys in Donnington Castle saw Waller move off to the north and endeavoured to attack his rearguard somewhere along the route but without much success; although he took twelve men captive, his attack caused little interference with Waller's progress. Curiously, it appears that Boys did not send word to Maurice of what he had seen, and although they were prepared for an attack on Speen, it seems Maurice's men were not warned that such an attack was already on its way.

Popular secondary accounts say that at daybreak on the 27th, Douglas and his Royalist grand guard at Boxford were attacked and quickly dispersed, some retreating to Newbury and others disappearing into the woodland. It is generally held that for all their warning they were ill-prepared and partially dispersed, and consequently were surprised and scattered. One disparaging historian has suggested that Douglas was so

The bridge and mill at Boxford where Douglas was surprised and failed to stop Waller's advance.

incompetent that he didn't even have scouts out. However, it is also known that Douglas left Donnington heading north not west, so perhaps he had intended to intercept Waller and slow his progress. The dismal show at Boxford may have been because there was only a small picket there, rather than his entire force of 500 men, Douglas having missed Waller during the night.

After crossing the Lambourne, Waller occupied a spine of high ground running parallel to the watercourse and divided his column. The Foot under Skippon, and presumably Balfour's Horse brigade, took the high road across Wickham Heath and through Stockcross (today the B4000), although some Horse must have continued south and then swung east on the Great West Road (now the A4). Meanwhile, Cromwell and his portion of the Eastern Association Horse worked their way along the valley bottom, through what is today Huntspeen and Woodspeen. All parts of the force converged before Speen at the eastern end of Wickham Heath. However, progress was slow; the men were tired after marching virtually all night and it was not until 1.00pm that the guns came up. At last, by 3.00pm they were all in position and deployed to attack. After clearing the area of some

Speenlawn, where Waller deployed to attack, is marked today by the A4 roundabout.

commanded muskets, Waller adopted a traditional formation, with Sir William Balfour's Horse on the right, Skippon's Foot in three great bodies in the centre with the light guns, and Cromwell's Horse on the left. He ordered the guns to be fired: this was the agreed signal to alert Manchester that he was ready and for him to launch his major attack – but Manchester's forces did not move.

Indeed, Manchester's forces in the east had had a hard day. They had been involved in fighting early that morning but their opening moves had been driven back, losing ground to Lisle's men. The Eastern Association Foot had quickly become dejected and morale was low. Time was short if a combined assault on the Royalists' position were to be effective and Waller could not wait, especially as Boys in Donnington had seen them and directed his guns their way, to add to those Maurice already had trained upon them. The fire from the castle could not have been as dangerous as some writers suggest since Boys only had four guns, but when added to those of Prince Maurice one can appreciate why Waller later wrote, 'Their cannon made our ground very hot . . . there was no way left but to fall on with Horse and Foot, and that without delay'. Nevertheless, it seems that it still took about 30 minutes to effect.

Unfortunately for the Royalists, it would appear that despite the ferocity of the fighting around Shaw, their central command understood Manchester's efforts to be a diversion, and believed his lack of movement in the late afternoon meant that the real battle would not take place until the next day, the 28th. Orders had been given to Maurice's regiments to 'stand down' and many of his cavalry reserve had actually dispersed to forage just before Waller's attack went in.

This attack was led by a 'forlorn hope' of Horse, possibly from Balfour's Brigade, who quickly overwhelmed their Royalist counterparts. Next went 800 musketeers, presumably attacking the ditches and other works of the Speenlawn barricade and its battery of guns. Led by W. Lloyd, Lieutenant-Colonel of Aldrich's Regiment, and Sergeant-Major Alexander Urrey from Robartes' Regiment, they exchanged volleys of shot with Maurice's commanded muskets until Lord-General Essex's Regiment of Foot came up on their right and forced the defenders to pull back. Lloyd was shot in the arm but his men surged forward.

The main assault upon the 400 men in the great barricade was launched by the four regiments in Aldrich's Brigade, with light artillery support from guns placed possibly in what was then Dean's Wood. Despite not being fully prepared, the so-called redoubt being unfinished, Maurice's men and close-range guns managed to throw the attackers back. The Cornish Horse made a desperate charge but its troopers were overwhelmed by the sheer numbers of Balfour's Horse and retired to Speenhamland, uncovering the position's left.

Aldrich's second advance managed to gain a foothold on the front of the barricade; the men clawed their way through, climbing over the dead and dying in the ditch. The barricade could not hold and was overrun as Essex's own regiment, profiting from the lack of cavalry cover, hooked into its left flank and stormed the position with 'great boldness'. Essex's old Foot tore into the embrasures and over the defences, and some say they were driven by sheer fury and hatred of the Cornish. The Royalist infantry and gunners fled and the jubilant Parliamentarians seized the five guns deployed in the battery. Ludlow says that Essex's men, who had been at Lostwithiel, recognised some of the pieces and embraced them with tears in their eyes, as if retaking them wiped out the shame of their surrender earlier in the year. One of the men killed in this action was Captain Gawler of the Lord-General's Regiment; a Glamorgan man, he had been taken prisoner in Cornwall but somehow rejoined the army. The retaken guns were turned and fired into the rear of the retreating Royalists.

Two City Regiments, the Red and the Yellow, moved up from the second

The crest of the ridge where the Lostwithiel guns once stood. Despite the incision of the A34 slip road, the rising ground is still discernable. The oak tree on the right also commemorates the unsuccessful fight to preserve the battle's heritage.

line to take over the position on the right vacated by Essex's Regiment's storm. The Red Regiment appears to have been held back while the Blue moved left to support Barclay. One answer to the lack of reported action concerning Waller's Foot was that they formed the Reserve, although this role seems to have been allocated to Harrington's London Brigade.

Some secondary sources state the success of this assault was probably due to the works not being completed. However, it is debatable whether the real cause was incomplete works or inadequate defence by the troops. Certainly Maurice's infantry included some of the Cornish Foot that had served so valiantly in the west, but by this time they were a long way from home, had been considerably reduced in number and had lost many of their original officers; added to this, their disgraceful behaviour towards their beaten foes at Lostwithiel had engendered great bitterness and hatred, which would only have fuelled the ferocity of the onslaught. Whether the Cornishmen were behind the barricade or on a rise to its right is unknown, but their presence would doubtless have inflamed Parliamentarian passions. In addition,

Speenlawn north. The A34 by-pass destroyed the site of the Royalist Horse's assaults on Barclay's Brigade, but the low land in the distance is where Cromwell's men advanced along the Lambourne.

Maurice's army was not a homogenous or a 'happy' force. Like Waller's, it was a composite of earlier armies and there was considerable enmity between the Cornishmen and the many Frenchmen who had enlisted in the Royalist cause. There had even been fighting between the two factions, especially at Bedminster, which was virtually burnt down in the fracas, and they certainly did not trust each other.

Waller had also ordered his Horse to fall on. On the south side, despite having driven off the Cornish Horse, Balfour's Brigade was prevented from fully taking part in the attack by the steepness of the slope of the spur as it fell away to the flooded watermeadows of the Kennet, but on the left Cromwell struggled forward through the enclosures to get into the more open fields. The Eastern Association Horse made slow progress with the Lambourne on their left flank, and soon came up to a deep ditch that proved difficult to cross – Cromwell had only got half his men over when they were attacked by 800 troopers of the Earl of Cleveland's Brigade of Horse, led by their General of Horse, George, Lord Goring. Details of this fight are scarce

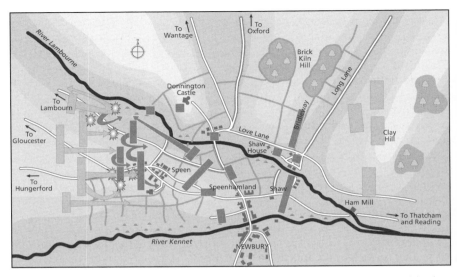

Map 13: Waller's forceful attack drove Maurice's men out of their works and back through Speen village.

but Cromwell's leading regiments, already disordered by the crossing of the ditch, were thrown into disarray and fell back. He managed to reinforce them and attacked while Goring's troopers were halted and trying to reorder, but it was to little avail. Middleton tried to stem the retreat but the Eastern Association men refused to either recognise or obey him. The Royalist accounts say the Eastern Association Horse were scattered in confusion. Had Cromwell broken through, and his men shown the fighting spirit they had displayed at Marston Moor, there may have been surprising results, especially as it seems the King himself was in this area and could have been taken if Cromwell had not retreated. Apologists argue that he was under the Donnington guns and in terrible cavalry country, but these guns were at long range and the ground was the same for both sides: there is no doubt that in this instance Cromwell's lack of drive cost the Parliamentarians dearly.

Seeing Cromwell's overthrow, Waller threw out a strong body of infantry to check the pursuit and afford the Eastern Association Horse an opportunity to rally. This body appears to have been part of Barclay's Brigade, which was also pressing forward against Maurice's Royalists north of Speen. Having disposed of Cromwell's Horse, Cleveland's Brigade now charged the Parliamentarian infantry in order to aid their own recoiling Foot. For a short while even Barclay's veterans were driven back by the ferocity of the Royalist onslaught. Major Urrey, who had led the initial attack with Lloyd, was shot in the head and captured by Captain Ellises of Colonel Richard Thornhill's Regiment of Horse, but he did not survive the day. Barclay's Brigade withstood three charges from the undaunted Royalist horse, until the Blue Regiment came from the Reserve to extend their left and provide more covering fire. Gradually the Foot, using the hedges and ditches, got the upper hand and the impetuous Goring was driven off with 'stinging pikes and a hail of bullets'. But they came on again and once again they drove into the Foot, despite being volleyed on the way in. They certainly penetrated the Parliamentarian line. Whether it was a deliberate tactic or not, it would appear that several parties of royal Horse passed through the ranks of Barclay's Foot, which then re-formed behind them, cutting off their retreat and subjecting them again to point-blank musketry. The plight of Goring's men also seems to have been exacerbated by some regrouped Eastern Association Horse attacking them too; these may have been the single troop or so that Middleton managed to inspire or perhaps they were from Essex's

Donnington Castle

The open ground over which Cromwell advanced. It is clearly within sight and range of the great southern bastion of Donnington Castle, although how much damage the guns positioned there could have caused is debatable.

army. Surrounded and trapped, the Royalist horsemen fought desperately but were slowly overwhelmed. Goring managed to cut his way out with a handful of followers and yet again ran the gauntlet of musketry before galloping away, but the Earl of Cleveland's horse was shot from under him and he was captured, apparently by a lieutenant from Colonel Henry Barclay's own Regiment of Foot. However, on both sides of the field the Royalist Horse had once again proven its superiority; certainly the majority of Cromwell's force appears to have quit the field, much to Manchester's later disgust.

On the high ground Maurice's second line put up a bloody resistance, with a lot of the hard fighting being done by the Duke of York's Regiment under William St Leger. The commanding officer of Robartes' Regiment, Lieutenant-Colonel William Hunter, fell. By 3.30pm the Royalist first line had been driven back by the advancing Parliamentarians with their battle cry of 'Forward! Forward!' and soon both sides were locked in house-to-house fighting in Speen itself. Cannon may have been dragged up to aid the clearance, as the author was shown a saker ball by a resident who had dug it out of her front garden. Local tradition has the church also being fought over but the current building is Victorian and offers no evidence. In about 30 minutes the barricaded heath and rise as well as Speen village fell to Skippon and the total of captured guns increased to nine, six of which were said to be sakers surrendered at Lostwithiel.

Although it is very unlikely that the royal standard was on Speen Moor, the royal headquarters might have been in the western portion of the whole position as Walker records that the King and his son Prince Charles were nearly captured when Speen was taken. The Parliamentarians burned for revenge for Lostwithiel and the barbaric treatment meted out to the unarmed and starving survivors by the Cornish Foot and the cry 'No Quarter!' was heard all around the field. The retreating Western Foot broke into a rout, shouting, 'Devils! Devils! They fight like Devils!' and fled past the King, who tried valiantly to stop them. They 'very basely forsook him and ran into Newbury', and it supposedly took the body of Foot stationed on the Kennet Bridge to halt them. For a while there must have been panic and confusion in Northbrook Street.

By 4.00pm the village was in Waller's hands and the Royalists were forced back towards Newbury, offering as they went a defiant defence from the various hedged enclosures. Amid these enclosures Waller himself had a narrow escape when he was assailed from behind by a Royalist trooper, whose deadly stroke he dodged before the man was killed, although whether Waller was with his Horse or Skippon's Foot at this juncture is unclear. We are told that Skippon kept up the pressure and gradually his three great bodies of Foot forced the Royalists to relinquish ditched hedge-line after ditched hedge-line until they came to the thick boundary hedge between Speen and Speenhamland, where the attack appears to have stalled.

The battle was now in full swing, and with Parliament's troops all accounted for and the Oxford road well protected by Boys in the castle, it would have made sense for a significant portion of the Reserve Foot under Blagge to march west to aid Maurice. Although such a move appears in several modern narratives, there is not much evidence for it from the primary sources. I believe that at this point parts of Blagge's Tertio were fed out towards both Speen and Shaw, while the rest remained in the central Reserve.

The fighting seems to have come to a stop across the Great West Road at what has since been dubbed by some historians as the 'Speenhamland Hedge'. The name Speenhamland seems to embrace a wide area with a 'movable' southern boundary! On some maps it is the Kennet, on others the Great West Road. The most likely location for this hedge seems to be somewhere in an arc north-west of Newbury cutting the main A4 road. According to Rocque there is no discernable unbroken hedge-line running roughly south-west–north-east, although one can be pieced together between Claypit and Horsepool Fields using the 1730 map in the town museum. To identify the hedge beyond doubt is impossible without major research, although we can hazard a guess that any force defending it would rest its flanks on the boggy ground of the Lambourne and the Kennet.

It is likely that several attacks were made on this hedge-line but reorganising after the first phase would have taken too long for a concerted assault to have been arranged, and even if Waller's Foot had been the Reserve they would have run out of daylight before they could be successfully fed forward through Speen village and deployed to attack. Some modern narratives say fighting was resumed but I have yet to be convinced. Instead I think the hedge saw a bloody stalemate. Hedges of this period, especially boundary hedges, were high and thick, layered and ditched to prevent determined cattle escaping through them. They soaked up the impetus of a pike charge and gave cover and a firing platform to musketeers, and although their bullet-stopping power was almost negligible they did help morale. Gaps could be cut in them, but with pikes jabbing across the top and muskets poking through the middle, almost into the faces of those on the far side, the obstacle became both a help and an uncrossable hindrance for both sides. It would seem, however, that Waller decided to try to outflank this deadlocked Foot conflict with his Horse, and ordered Cromwell to push forward on his wing, anchoring his left on the Lambourne, while Balfour was to do likewise on the Kennet side. Now having access to gentler slopes, Balfour swept around the south of Speen church, but Cromwell did not move. The Royalists were deployed in reasonably open fields but Balfour

The patchwork of small enclosures south of Speen which Balfour's Horse had to cross.

had to reach their formations through a patchwork of smaller enclosures.

As well as being baulked by the hedges, Balfour's men found the normally marshy ground near the Kennet was flooded. Progress was slow. About 4.15pm, with daylight already fading, Balfour managed to exploit a gateway into a larger open field far over on the right, the task being made easier by the presence of some commanded muskets. He was met by Sir Humphrey Bennet's Brigade of Horse, from which a body under Major William Legge rode forward to attack them. The Royalists used their ground to perform a proper advance, in ordered ranks, gradually increasing speed and momentum, yet Balfour's men, disordered and from a standing start, counter-charged in a somewhat piecemeal fashion, and unexpectedly repelled them. Falling back, Legge's riders did more damage to their own brigade than they had to Balfour's, as several other troops decided to quit the field with them and Bennet found his brigade beginning to disintegrate around him. He did manage to rally a significant portion of them, but legend has it that some rode pell-mell back into Newbury and once again the Foot on the Kennet Bridge had to stop a rout and turn them around. Northbrook Street may not have seen any fighting but it certainly saw some action.

Today this is Goldwell Park, but in 1644 it was probably the open field down which Stuart charged to prevent Balfour from capturing the King.

However, their flight had opened the door to Newbury and left the King's small mounted party alone in the open field, at the mercy of any adventuresome troop of Balfour's victorious Horse.

Some musketeers among the hedges and ditches on the southern flank prevented Balfour from following up his initial victory. However, much of the Royalist cavalry must have been within easy supporting distance of this reversal because we are told that Her Majesty the Queen's Regiment of Horse under Sir John Cansfield, from Lord Wentworth's Brigade of Horse, came to their aid, and stemmed the Parliamentarian advance. They were seconded by Lord Bernard Stuart, brother of the Duke of Richmond and Lennox, leading His Majesty the King's Lifeguard of Horse, which first surrounded their monarch and then wheeled and fell on Balfour's flank. These two regiments, supposedly supported by the rest of Wentworth's brigade, drove Balfour back. Meanwhile Bennet's errant troopers had been rounded up, some believe by a sort of Provost, and sent back to join their comrades. Once re-formed, Bennet's Brigade apparently took over from Wentworth's, which seems to have been shifted to the eastern sector almost immediately afterwards; it is not far. Bennet's men redeemed their honour

The path of Bennet's Brigade's flight. The church is in the centre of Newbury.

by finally driving the Parliamentarian Horse back beyond the hedge-line, where Skippon hastily organised a defence with his pikemen, held them, and then, assisted by musketeers, beat them back. Sir Edward Waldegrave's Regiment of Horse must have been in the thick of this action for they lost both Captain Catlyn and the son of the commanding officer, Captain Waldegrave, who was seriously wounded.

FALSE CLAIMS

As part of the propaganda war contemporary accounts often claimed their men had killed leading enemy officers. For example, on one occasion *Mercurius Aulicus* refuted the *Parliamentarian Letter*'s story that Goring's brother Charles had been shot dead and added, 'General Goring's brother is ready for another Charge when the Rebels next appear.' However, earlier in the same news-sheet it states that the commanding officer of Essex's Lifeguard, supposedly Charles Doyley, had been shot and killed by Bennet, whereas in fact Doyley was unharmed and indeed survived the war.

The stand-off at Speenhamland Hedge continued. Balfour seems to have rallied his men and re-formed, switching several regiments to the left to replace Cromwell's men. As at Newbury I, they had been beaten but not destroyed and were ready to go into action again if need be. Aware that they constituted the only Horse the King now had, Goring and Maurice were loathe to commit their troopers to a general attack on both flanks as Waller had done, so from about 4.30pm the cavalry of both sides rested, while in the centre Skippon's, Maurice's and Blagge's Foot watched each other. We can suppose some regiments were brought up to replace tired ones, and muske-teers were taken out of the line every so often to reload at the budge barrels or collect refilled collars. The stalemate lasted until the early evening, when Waller drew off his exhausted troops at about 5.00pm. He did not, however, allow them to retire far and they occupied the erstwhile Royalist quarters at Speen. Despite their weariness they were in good heart and readied them-selves for a renewed assault on the hedge in the morning.

Manchester and the East

Having seen Waller safely off on his outflanking march, Manchester settled down for the night but rose early to supervise the deployment of his

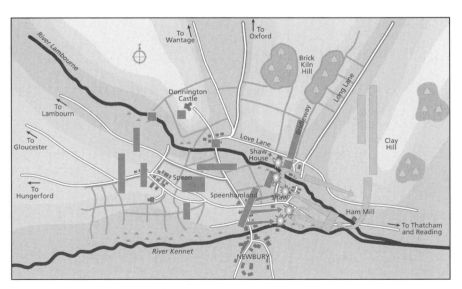

Map 14: Manchester's early morning attack was intended to draw attention away from Waller's activities to the west.

diversionary attack on Shaw village and Shaw House. Whether he got much sleep is debatable as orders were given to keep up a sporadic fire on the Royalist positions to focus their attention on this sector of the field. In the east the initiative lay completely with Manchester and at dawn, roughly 7.00 am, on the morning of the 27th he deployed his Foot in four large bodies on the western slopes of Clay Hill with Ludlow's 1,500 Horse on their left. We do not know where the dragoons were. Initially Manchester's own regiment might have been the Reserve. Lord Astley was in no hurry to begin the action for with every passing hour his defences grew stronger as his men laboured on their construction. However, both sides' guns opened up and parties of Parliamentarian commanded musketeers were ordered down Clay Hill to probe various parts of the line.

Shortly after 7.00am Manchester launched his diversionary attack. Three bodies of Foot moved forward from the east, advancing across the slopes of Clay Hill. A fourth body went south of the Lambourne as they 'put a tertia of foot over a bridge which they had made in the night' near Ham Mill about a mile to the east, probably near the broken-down main road bridge. Shrouded by early morning mist and hidden by folds in the ground, this force managed to cross the flooded river meadows and was almost on top of

The modern bridge over the Lambourne in Shaw. The mill is to the left.

Shaw Mill has been considerably altered from the building that witnessed fighting during both attacks.

the Royalist defences before the men were seen. They were perhaps aided by the Royalist assumption that the ground was too wet for an attack to be launched across it, which meant they were lax in patrolling it. They fell on and took two works, driving on into Shaw village, where there was significant fighting around the mill. Some small parties, carried away with their success, even penetrated the Royalist line, crossing over the Lambourne, possibly over a footbridge near the mill and the site of today's modern bridge, and pressed on into the grounds of Shaw House where they assaulted the buildings.

In the house Lisle reacted quickly. Musketry was brisk from both sides, but the attack was stemmed and held all along the southern half of the line. The men who had got through were finally repelled with losses and the whole attack was checked by Sir Bernard Astley who brought forward a force of 400 musketeers from his reserve position. Diversionary attacks are not meant to escalate into serious engagements and those taking part usually fall back in good order. However, in getting into the village (never mind the party that penetrated the Royalist line and reached Shaw House) this one was over-committed and sustained heavier casualties than expected. The whole body fell back in disorder the way it came, with some groups keeping on the north bank of the Lambourne while others from the southern sector peeled northwards and tried to get over the river wherever they could. Royalist sources say some men were drowned although the depth of the water makes this questionable, even allowing for an unmanaged river in a wet season. During the retreat many men panicked and ran headlong into the waiting units of their own men who were preparing to make the main attack later in the day, causing serious disruption. The whole wing had to fall back up Clay Hill under the protection of their cannon to regroup. It was a disastrous beginning for the Parliamentarian assault. Bernard Astley's men picked up over 200 arms and 'a great store of pillage', including a number of buffcoats that were stripped from casualties; this prompted two Royalist accounts to state that the London regiments had taken part in the assault.

Much of the rest of the morning was spent in long-range cannonading and desultory skirmishing. Astley ordered nothing that would precipitate the fighting, while Manchester simply waited until late in the afternoon, long after the time at which Waller was supposed to assault Maurice. Why he waited has been the subject of much historical debate, but he himself said he was expecting reinforcements from Reading and that he had not heard the signal to march forward, the sound of Waller's guns opening fire on Speen having been drowned out by the noise of his own guns' preparatory bombardment and those of Shaw House replying.

After the initial fighting Lord Astley requested 400 musketeers from Blagge's Reserve and allocated them to Lisle, who put them as a fresh garrison into Shaw House. Whether he withdrew any of the original 1,000, and what he did with them if he did, remains unknown. Their cavalry support, His Royal Highness Charles, Prince of Wales's Regiment of Horse under Sir John Browne and a party of Prince Rupert's Dragoons commanded by Sir Thomas Hooper, moved forward into the open fields on the gentle slopes below Brick-kiln Copse, to the left of Shaw House. Several of Bernard Astley's units now occupied Shaw village in strength, but Jacob Astley still kept some of them, along with some regiments of Lisle's, as his Reserve, although how many or which regiments we are not told, except that one was Thelwell's, who seems to have also had command of the whole body. Later, to counter Manchester's main attack, the rest of Lord Wentworth's Brigade of Horse came over from the west and formed up in a field near Shaw church.

The main attack was finally launched between 4.00 and 4.15pm.

Manchester sent two large bodies of troops forward in a two-pronged assault concentrating on the northern sector of Lord Astley's position. One body headed for the fields north of Shaw House, while the other sought to attack the house itself and also to force the gap between it and Shaw village. This twin attack was supported by the Horse under Ludlow, and some writers argue that there was also a move to threaten the gap between Shaw village and the northern suburbs of Newbury. There is little evidence for the composition of the attack. It would have made sense to keep in reserve the force that had been mauled in the morning's attack, although some historians say that these men drove some Royalist outposts off the north bank and crossed the Lambourne again, this time contenting themselves with pinning Sir Bernard Astley's Tertio in place, thus preventing it from coming to Lisle's aid. This would have meant that one of the attacks, probably the southern one, was seriously down on numbers.

The royal troops faced east and braced themselves as the attackers streamed over Clay Hill and down its slopes, singing psalms as they advanced. As the northernmost body approached the Royalist line they were

The line of march of Manchester's Right, down Clay Hill towards that part of Astley's line that extended north of Shaw. Long Lane is in the middle-ground while the Curridge bridleway is further up the slope.

met by a forlorn hope of 40 commanded musketeers among the hedges, probably in Long Lane. Some of Manchester's force must have come across what is now the cemetery. Overwhelming the commanded musketeers, they crossed the road and entered the fields on a direct collision course with the main Royalist line now dug in among the hedges. The clash came at a strongly held hedge, which can perhaps be interpreted as the Curridge bridleway. Lisle's men bravely held their fire until they could deliver a full volley, which crashed out and stopped the Parliamentarians in their tracks. They faltered, but soon recovered and pressed on, launching an assault on the hedge-line. This was thrown back and a firefight developed while Manchester's men re-formed and some light guns were brought up to support their attack; cannon and musket balls have been found in this area. The Eastern Association Foot attacked again, and again they were repulsed. This was repeated several times until eventually, with the support of Ludlow's cavalry, they forced their way through the hedge-line by sheer weight of numbers and won possession of the lane and its twin hedges. They celebrated 'with a great shout', and then continued their assault, swarming up and over the hedges and works and into the enclosures beyond.

The Curridge bridleway was held by Lisle's Left. Residents tell of musket balls being found in the fields on both sides.

The north garden wall of Shaw House overlooking Love Lane. From this protected position Royalist musketeers poured fire into Ludlow's troopers both in the fields opposite and in the lane itself.

The mêlée became general, with pikes, swords and butts, but the attackers continued to surge forward, cresting the spur of Brick-kiln Hill. There they were presumably harassed by Hooper's dragoons and then checked by a charge from the Prince of Wales's Regiment of Horse led by Sir John Browne; it would appear that the Queen's and the King's Lifeguard of Horse, having switched flanks from the west, also came into the line. Outflanked, the Parliamentarian Foot were forced to defend an enclosure. Ludlow quickly committed his cavalry to take the pressure off the Foot. The Queen's withstood their charge and were soon reinforced by the Lifeguards, at which point Ludlow's cavalry wheeled away. Nearer the house, after a sharp engagement the Prince of Wales's Regiment was obliged to retire. The Royalist Foot fell back too. The Reserve had earlier been brought up and part of it fed into Shaw House gardens, where the retreating men found sanctuary among them. Browne's troopers withdrew far enough for their muskets on the north wall of the garden of Shaw House to give them covering fire.

At the time this wall sat upon the raised earth banks of the sunken Love

Lane and some of Ludlow's Horse must have been caught packed in a point-blank death-trap. Some of the attackers from this northern attack seem to have become mixed up with those of the southern force and they both surged around an isolated hillock lying between the house and Long Lane. With fire coming into their left flank, some of it from the leather guns which both Gwyn and Birch say Page had as part of the House defences, Ludlow's men reined in, turned and began to retire. Browne quickly organised his own 'about face' and then charged again, this time into their rear. The Lifeguards too gave chase, converting this retirement into a retreat. However, these exertions had taken their toll and now, somewhat spent and completely disordered, the Royalist Horse no longer posed a serious threat to the massed Foot, especially as they now sought shelter behind hedges, but the gallant Royalist horsemen had bought valuable time and taken ground from the enemy cavalry; they held this ground for the remainder of the battle, albeit under occasional musket fire, one such shot killing Mr Jones of the King's Troop.

Ludlow's Horse may have been forced back, but the Foot was still there. Lisle had to counter this portion of the attack, so he called Thelwell forward with 300 muskets from his Reserve. They were joined by other bodies of

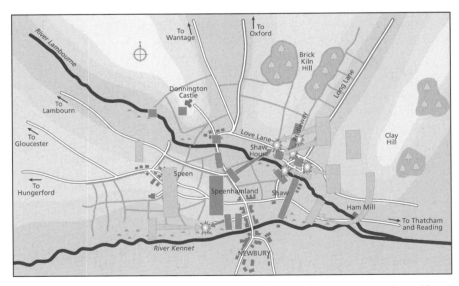

Map 15: Finally, as the light faded, Manchester launched his main assault on Shaw House while Waller and Blagge disputed the boundary hedge and the Royalist Horse drove their counterparts back.

muskets, presumably those thrown out of the bridleway, and also by the surviving men of the forlorn hope that had been ousted from Long Lane earlier. 'Shot flew extream on both sides' and after firing several punishing volleys, Thelwell's men clubbed muskets and fell on with the butt. They stormed forward and drove their foe back to the bridleway hedge. Climbing and scrambling over it, they fought on, keeping Manchester's men on the retreat until they had cleared them out of the field and secured the further hedge, once more occupying Long Lane and forming a line with the hillock. They also secured a number of prisoners, one of Crawford's colours (indicating that the Crawford/Hobart brigade must have been part of that force) and a couple of light guns; it was their turn to give a 'great shout' in celebration.

The Shaw House attack was directed at the north-east corner of the buildings and was met by stern resistance. The attack got hung up on the left by a large breastwork dug into a small hillock on the rise above Shaw village, in between the house and Long Lane. It was a commanding position and difficult to assault because of the hillock's steep and fortified face. Royalist sources boast that although they attacked several times that day, no enemy

Shaw Lane rises up a hillock as it goes north. On the left, at its height, the Royalists'
untaken work was to disrupt the attacks on the house.

The houses of Shaw north of the Lambourne. This crossroads and its buildings were furiously fought over and changed hands several times.

soldiers got on to the hillock and lived, other than as prisoners. This hillock remained in Royalist hands during the action, although the Parliamentarians must have swept round either side of it.

However, the Royalist line broke again between Lisle's and Bernard Astley's Tertios and the Parliamentarians swept forward, ousting the defenders of the few buildings in Shaw village on the north bank of the Lambourne and then driving on to assault the works around the east wall of the house.

A singular incident occurred before the fighting for the buildings began. *Mercurius Aulicus* describes a lone Parliamentarian officer approaching the defences and ordering those in the house and gardens not to shoot. Whether he was trying to parley without a drummer or even a white flag is unknown, but Page ordered his men to fire and the officer was shot in the belly. General shooting then broke out, with Lisle's men making good use of their cover and defensive works. The many windows of Shaw House are said to have bristled with musket barrels which poured fire into the Parliamentarians as they struggled forward, trying to return fire while clambering across the palisades, pulling down the sharpened stakes and scaling the banks and barricades of the works.

In all probability Royalist musketeers were also positioned on the roof and in the loft spaces, from where they would have fired through holes knocked in the tiles. We are told they fired as fast as they could, which possibly meant three rounds per minute. Manchester's men actually got into the gardens of the house, and indeed came close to the main building as some of the men from the northern 'column' joined them on the front lawn. Concentrated close-range fire from the house and the dry moat, where a large body of muskets supported by leather guns had been concealed, inflicted crippling losses on the attackers, who also came under fire from musketeers behind the hedges in the lane near the old rectory; they were forced to fall back. Another Royalist 'great shout' rent the air, and Lisle then took the offensive.

In this counter-attack he is reputed to have been at the head of three infantry charges, leading the first with the cry 'For the Crown!' His second charge went in with the shout 'For Prince Charles!' and the third 'For the Duke of York!' Lisle is later credited with saying that he would have gone

Shaw House itself was occupied by Page under Lisle's command and proved to be an important bastion for the Royalist defence of Newbury.

The north-east embankments and corner of Shaw House where the attack supposedly broke through.

through the entire royal family if he had to! Lisle was noted as a man who seldom wore armour but he is also said to have cast aside his buffcoat in the heat of the action. Some writers have ascribed this to his wish to be seen by his men, while others state that this was a Royalist recognition symbol and all his command followed suit. No matter what the correct version, it certainly must have been hot work as they captured some colours and numerous prisoners and overran several guns.

We are told that during this attack part of the Parliamentarian southern force came under fire on its flank as it marched up to join the fray. Who was responsible for this remains uncertain. It could have been that one of Lisle's counter-attacks spilled to its right, or perhaps it was the work of another portion of the Reserve, as evidence suggests that at some stage in the fighting Colonel Anthony Thelwell's Regiment of Foot, probably led by their lieutenant-colonel, was brought up and stationed behind more hedges near the old rectory, between the house and the river crossing in Shaw village. Alternatively it may have been musketeers from Astley's brigade from across the Lambourne, pouring fire into the flank of the men as they moved along the river's north bank. Perhaps it was all three! But no matter who fired the shots, the supports were surprised and hurt and the attack failed as they too retreated from the fray.

The Royalists were just too well dug in. By now, the light was going and the attackers had already lost about 500 men. All along the line of Long Lane Lisle's regiments drove the Parliamentarians back and then tried to storm Clay Hill. They failed, but in the southern sector Bernard Astley's men left their defences and succeeded in securing the hedges on the far side of the Lambourne, presumably taking Ham Mill as well, thus making another Parliamentarian attack even more difficult. The Parliamentarian regiments withdrew under cover of a supporting action led by Ludlow, and the commanded musketeers from both sides settled in to a firefight among the hedges all along the line, much as had happened in the west. Page himself must have left the safety of the house, as during these final exchanges he was wounded three times, with one ball in the arm and one in each thigh! In the twilight Manchester sent a party of Horse to gather the guns that had been abandoned, but they came under fire and withdrew. Sunset prevented any further attacks, and night saw Manchester draw off; like Waller, he did not retire very far. With his superiority in numbers, he too intended to renew the battle in the morning.

Newbury II, like Newbury I, stuttered to a close with both sides breathing heavily and glad of the respite, although yet again in the Parliamentarian camps spirits were higher and the two commanders felt confident of victory the next day.

Afterwards

Casualties in the fighting were heavy, but roughly even. They were estimated at around 500 killed on each side but these figures were issued by the respective armies and are probably too low. As the attackers, the number of Parliament's killed and wounded must have exceeded those of the King. The Royalist dead included Anthony St Leger, Lieutenant-Colonel Leak and Colonel Topping, and among the wounded were the Lord-General, the Earl of Brentford, Sir John Grenville, Sir John Cansfield and Major Alford. The dead were buried in grave-pits near where they fell, and those who died of their wounds in Newbury were interred in St Nicholas's churchyard.

It is thought that a hastily called Council of War sealed the Royalists' fate. Charles knew that his losses made the outnumbering ratio against them even greater, and he had lost one of his three main strong-points. He was not in a position to attack and retake Speen, and the numbers would inevitably tell at Speenhamland Hedge. His forces were fighting on two fronts and becoming vulnerable; to continue fighting would only delay the inevitable. He had to retreat and save as much of his army as he could. Thus, of his own volition or because he was pressed to do so by his senior officers, as happened later at Naseby, Charles quit the field. Under the cover of night, at about 1.00am, he abandoned his army and rode for Bath, taking his Lifeguard of Horse with him and leaving Prince Maurice to shift as best he could to get the army out.

Maurice made prodigious efforts that night. Using the trick Waller had used at Lansdown, he ordered his men to leave lighted match on walls and in bushes to fool the enemy into believing that they were still in position, while they gradually withdrew, unit after unit, towards the centre and then up the Oxford road. Maurice managed to get the royal army through a gap less than 1,000m wide between Waller's and Manchester's forces. Regiment after regiment crossed the Lambourne without mishap. A lot of the cavalry had to swim across, and indeed some of the Foot had to wade as the wagons, guns and carriages took precedence for using the little bridge in Donnington village. Maurice also got the guns and the wounded, including Lord-General Ruthven, up the hill and into the relative safety of the castle and its works, where they were left with Boys while the rest of the army made a hasty retreat towards Oxford. The redeemed Bennet's Brigade had the honour of providing the rearguard, and a hundred of them even remained scouting and probing until dawn. In the morning Ruthven slipped out of the castle and rode for Bath, and Boys' guns fired on the Parliamentarians in some sort of derisory salute.

The Parliamentarians occupied Newbury while a Council dispute raged: Manchester had little wish to send a force towards Bath after the King, whose capture he could not countenance. In addition, although a pursuit of Maurice was ordered by Waller, it was poorly executed. Cromwell chased them for 2½ miles but was recalled by Manchester. A later and more organised follow-up was ordered, and this time Cromwell got as far as Harwell near Didcot before deciding to give up, blaming the restricted nature of the lanes beyond Abingdon which would impede his wagons. Maurice got away via Compton, reaching Wallingford and crossing the Thames. Cromwell returned to Newbury. A somewhat desultory attack was later made on Donnington Castle but this too was badly done and easily repulsed. There was a late move north in strength with the intention of forcing the issue with Maurice but by that time he had been reinforced from Oxford and the King had met with Rupert in Bath and had begun marching towards their flank. The Parliamentarians regrouped, resupplied and reordered back at Newbury, Cromwell and his Horse being billeted in and around East Woodhay, and once again Donnington Castle was put under siege.

By 5 November the King had rejoined his army, bringing with him not only Rupert's forces from Bristol, but Northampton's brigade from Banbury

A FAMOUS QUARREL

When the Parliamentarians heard of the King's impending return to Newbury they hastily convened a council of war in a small house in Shaw Field. The meeting was dominated by irrelevant concerns about more French troops coming to England and by personal recriminations. In this acrimonious atmosphere, the following exchange was recorded:

Manchester: 'If we beat the King ninety-nine times, yet he is King still, and so will his posterity be after him. But if the King beat us once we shall all be hanged and our posterity be made slaves.'

Cromwell: 'If this be so, why did we take up arms at first? This is against fighting ever hereafter. If so, let us make peace be it never so base!'

Cromwell then accused his commanding officer of undermining the war effort and of treachery to the cause. It was a quarrel that prompted a government enquiry.

(which town he had successfully relieved with the aid of some Foot from the Oxford garrison led by Gage); in addition, more reinforcements arrived under Gerard and Langdale, and they held a grand review at Bullington Green. The King's army, so soon after its mauling at Newbury II, was once again a formidable force. Rupert had been returned to favour and replaced the wounded Ruthven as Lord-General; Ruthven became Lord Chamberlain to the Prince of Wales. Revitalised and supposedly some 15,000 strong, the army now marched south. Manchester ordered works to be dug facing north and batteries to be constructed, and Cromwell was instructed to throw the Eastern Association Horse against the advancing enemy, but the horses themselves were exhausted, having not been properly fed for weeks, and were in no condition to engage. These might also be the reasons why Cromwell's force had put up such a poor showing during the battle.

On 9 November the Royalists not only relieved Donnington once more, but deployed to offer battle at Speenhamland, the very ground from which they had skulked away only a fortnight before. While the royal army arrayed itself (for which deployment we do have a diagrammatic order of battle drawn by de Gomme), the guns and wounded were evacuated from the castle, repairs undertaken and supplies stocked in its cellars. The Parliamentarian command showed an unusual lack of zest for battle, refusing to be drawn out and instead sitting tight in their works and barricades. In their defence, their still-scattered mounted troops were only now rendezvousing on Wash Common, and although they began riding through Newbury and over the Kennet in an attempt to support any deployment, it became obvious they would arrive too late. The Royalists began a limited attack with both Horse and Foot on the part of the line held by Essex's men, who fired volleys into them and drove them off; as they pulled back, Captain Horsey led a party of commanded muskets after them to push them all the way back to their own lines, which seem to have been near Shaw House, between the house itself and Newbury. The Queen's Regiment of Horse was again involved and advanced with Prince Maurice's Horse in support, but their opposite numbers wheeled away and retired behind their guns and muskets, which fired on the Royalists, killing and wounding several, including Captain Fitzmaurice of the Prince's Regiment. The King himself must have been nearby as his horse was shot in the foot as he stood at the head of his own regiment. The rest of the royal army watched, then stood down, marching off with trumpets, drums and colours and followed by a few 'snipers'. The King spent the night in Donnington Castle while his army slept in the surrounding villages and fields.

The next day the weather was very bad but the Royalists offered battle again. According to the Calendar of State Papers this time the Parliamentarian Foot answered the challenge and began deploying on

Speenhamland from Donnington Castle. The open land in the middle-ground (now the golf course) is where Cromwell and Goring clashed.

Speenhamland in the rain. We do not know if this really took place, or was just a piece of clever propaganda to bolster the Parliamentarian morale. In the event no attack came, doubtless much to the relief of the Parliamentarian army, which was now in a poor state: the men had been long on campaign, had marched great distances in appalling conditions and had suffered a number of reverses, and they were only now recovering from the recent battle. Waller and Manchester held an argumentative and fractious Council of War and decided to withdraw from the field and not accept the Royalist challenge to 'Newbury III'.

The King similarly had no great desire to fight again, especially as he knew the defensive advantages of the field and had seen at first hand the strength of the new Parliamentarian works, so the Royalists marched away back to Oxford, via Lambourne. En route Rupert laid a trap for the pursuing Parliamentarians, stationing some Horse in a barn from which they burst forth, ambushing and killing fifteen enemy troopers. The royal army then returned to its base, happy that it had inflicted a moral defeat on their foes and gained a satisfactory end to a successful campaign; better still, both Banbury and Donnington had been reprovisioned and were still in their hands. Parliament and the Committee of Both Kingdoms were angered and frustrated by their commanders' futile efforts to ensnare the King and destroy his army when they had had every opportunity of doing so. Recriminations abounded. Manchester accused Waller of being hesitant and Cromwell of being not fully committed to fighting, and blamed them for causing the failure of the western attack. Waller accused Manchester of being late at the rendezvous and in launching his attack, thus undermining the plan to draw a significant part of the royal reserve his way. Both blamed Essex, intimating that he had feigned illness to avoid the battle. Cromwell blamed all three.

Summary

Strategically the King's campaign intentions were only partially realised. Two of the three besieged garrisons had been relieved but the piecemeal destruction of Parliament's forces before they could unite had not been achieved, nor had the occupation of winter quarters in East Anglia. The campaign fought by Manchester, Waller and Essex was reactive rather than planned, but they had thwarted the majority of the King's intentions and their efforts can be considered successful, if not well thought through nor gloriously executed. From the middle to the end of the 1644 campaign season they had achieved little of strategic advantage.

Newbury II was one of the few battles of the English Civil War in which an army attempted a wide outflanking move. Some analysts have cited this encircling flank march as an imaginative piece of tactical brilliance, while others condemn it as an act of extreme folly that miraculously paid off. Waller and Manchester took a considerable risk in dividing their army, but they were well aware that they enjoyed a marked superiority of numbers. Had Manchester's main attack been launched at the correct time, the outcome of the battle could have been very different. Indeed, this is one of the great 'what if' questions of military history. Similarly, what if Cromwell had driven forward, captured the King and routed Maurice before Blagge's Reserve could come to their aid? In the final analysis, the outnumbered King's army had fought Parliament's to a standstill and still held most of their ground. However, their Left had been driven in, Maurice's regiments had been soundly beaten and the Reserve had been committed. It is extremely unlikely that they could have survived a second day's fighting, whereas Waller's and Manchester's men were quite capable of renewing their assaults the next morning. Technically they had won the battle but then lost the initiative and their sense of purpose through political, denominational and deeply personal wrangling.

It is said that Cromwell's disgust was so great that it influenced him to make his complaint to the House against military commanders having personal agendas and the pitfalls of them holding political office, which resulted in the famous Self-Denying Ordinance with its remarkable and far-reaching effects.

Chapter Six

ORDERS OF BATTLE

Some historians accuse battlefield students of being too obsessed with battle orders and insist that moves made and ground occupied are far more important. This may be so, but knowing which troops performed which deeds is also important to the story of any battle. Knowing that Skippon used his Reserve to plug a gap in his line at Newbury I is adequate, but a much fuller appreciation of the situation and the event can be attained by understanding that he used two Militia units of Londoners. Who they were makes their feat even more interesting owing to their lack of experience. So, constructing battle orders is very worthwhile, and it is a fascinating pastime in its own right.

No definitive battle orders for either battle of Newbury have been discovered or completely reconstructed for either side. Regrettably, there is still not enough contemporary evidence, although relevant documents and accounts can offer important information. For example, in Byron's description of the fighting in which his uncle's tertio was involved, he names the King's Lifeguard, the Prince of Wales's (Woodhouse's) and the Lord General's. Such details can be compared to known formations both before and after the action for brigade continuity, for where contemporary evidence does not exist it may be reasonable to suppose that brigades were not dramatically reorganised during a campaign season, and thus lists relating to previous battles in the same year may be useful, even though such comparisons rest entirely on speculation. Another problem lies with the practice of drawing upon garrisons for detachments to join the field army temporarily; in such cases a unit cited as present could be either a full regiment or just one company or troop. It is often more difficult to discover the names and brigading of regiments among the Horse, as they were raised by troop, and although the practice of allocating six certain troops to a particular regiment was becoming established it was not yet permanent. A typical problem is with the royal Horse at Newbury I; we have a good idea which regiments were present but know virtually nothing about their brigade allocation. Similarly we know that several detachments of Foot from Newcastle's Army had escorted the Queen's convoy to Oxford and that they too were at Newbury. However, as small groups they were probably amalgamated into one unit but whether they served with Byron in the Oxford Brigade or with Vavasour is not certain. For Newbury II, we know that each tertio of Foot was sub-divided into three brigades, although we have no information as to which units constituted these sub-divisions. Fortunately some Parliamentarian records for both engagements are clearer, but difficulties still exist, such as understanding the role of unbrigaded regiments.

The information presented below is drawn from both contemporary sources and from both published and unpublished work by other researchers, several of whom disagree dramatically and scornfully. As a result, difficult choices have had to be made in the compiling of this list, so please treat it with caution. As with most battle orders of this period, the lists may not be complete and they contain by necessity a lot of speculation and probable error, although they represent 'my best deductions' from the current evidence.

Newbury I ORDER OF BATTLE PARLIAMENTARIAN

Lord General Robert Devereux, Earl of Essex
Lieutenant General of Horse Sir Philip Stapleton
Sergeant Major-General of Foot Philip Skippon
General of Ordnance Sir John Merrick

Right Wing: Lord Gen. Robert Devereux, Earl of Essex
First Line
Lt-Gen. Sir Philip Stapleton's Brigade of Horse:
    Earl of Essex's Lifeguard Troop of Horse (Robert Hammond)
    Earl of Essex's Regiment of Horse
    Lt-Gen. Sir William Balfour's Regiment of Horse (Balfour absent)
    Col. John Dalbier's Regiment of Horse
    Col. Arthur Goodwin's Regiment of Horse (Gilbert Blare)
    Col. Edmund Harvey's Regiment of Horse (City of London Horse)
    Col. Richard Norton's Regiment of Horse
    Col. Sir James Ramsey's Regiment of Horse
    Scout Master General Sir Samuel Luke's Regiment of Horse (3 troops)
    Capt. Jeremiah Abercrombie's Dragoons (1 company)
    Capt. Cornelius Shibborne's Dragoons (1 company)

Second Line
Sgt Maj.-Gen. James Holborne's Brigade of Foot:
   Sgt Maj.-Gen. James Holborne's Regiment of Foot
   Col. George Langham's Regiment of Foot
   Col. Francis Thompson's Regiment of Foot
Col. Henry Barclay's Brigade of Foot:
   Col. Henry Barclay's Regiment of Foot
   Col. John Holmstead's Regiment of Foot
   Col. Thomas Tyrell's Regiment of Foot
Unbrigaded:*
   Earl of Essex's Regiment of Foot (John Bamfield)

Centre and Left Wing: Sgt Maj.-Gen. Philip Skippon
Centre First Line
Sgt Maj.-Gen. Philip Skippon's Brigade of Foot:
   Col. Sir William Brooke's Regiment of Foot
   Col. Sir Henry Bulstrode's Regiment of Foot
   Sgt Maj.-Gen. Philip Skippon's Regiment of Foot
Centre Second Line
Unbrigaded:*
   Col. Sir William Springate's Regiment of Infantry
Left Wing First Line
   Sgt Maj. Richard Fortescue's Commanded Muskets
Left Wing Second Line
Col. John, Lord Robartes' Brigade of Foot:
   Col. Sir William Constable's Regiment of Foot
   Col. Francis Martin's Regiment of Foot
   Col. John, Lord Robartes' Regiment of Foot
Lt-Gen. John Middleton's Brigade of Horse:
   Lt-Gen. John Middleton's Regiment of Horse
   Col. Hans Behre's Regiment of Horse
   Col. Bazil Fielding, Earl of Denbigh's Regiment of Horse
   Col. Lord Grey of Groby's Regiment of Horse
   Col. Sir John Meldrum's Regiment of Horse
   Col. James Sheffield's Regiment of Horse

---

*   Unbrigaded regiments were not usual unless they were set aside for specific tasks. The Lord General's Regiment of Foot was similar in strength to the other two infantry brigades in the wing. The size of Springate's has not yet been discovered.

Reserve
Sgt Maj.-Gen. Randall Mainwaring's City of London Brigade of Foot:
  Sgt Maj.-Gen. Randall Mainwaring's Regiment of Foot
  The Red Regiment, London Trained Bands (William Tucker)
  The Blue Regiment, London Trained Bands (Francis West)*
  The Red Regiment, City of London Auxiliaries (Samuel Harsnett)
  The Blue Regiment, City of London Auxiliaries (John Warner)
  The Orange Regiment, City of London Auxiliaries (Thomas Gower)
Ordnance: Gen. of the Ordnance Sir John Merrick
The Field Battery of Artillery**
Sir John Merrick's Company of Firelocks

The Parliamentarian train consisted of two demi-culverins and twenty light
guns including drakes. Essex had left most of his heavier guns in Gloucester
to aid the defence of the city. He seems also to have had with him a few
medium guns that formed the battery on Round Hill, but his twenty or so
light pieces were, according to period practice, probably spread along the
line to accompany the Foot and increase their firepower.

Newbury I   ORDER OF BATTLE   ROYALIST

Captain General Charles Stuart, King of England
Lord General Patrick Ruthven, Earl of Forth
General of Horse Prince Rupert of the Rhine
Lieutenant General of Horse Henry, Lord Wilmot
Sergeant Major-General of Foot Sir Jacob Astley, assisted by Colonel
Nicholas Byron
General of the Ordnance Colonel Henry, Lord Percy

Right Wing: Sir William Vavasour
First Line
Col.-Gen. Sir William Vavasour's Tertio:
  Col. Edward, Lord Herbert's Regiment of Foot (Edward Somerset)
  Col.-Gen. Sir William Vavasour's Regiment of Foot
  Col. Sir Samuel Sandys' Regiment of Foot
  Col. Sir Anthony Mansell's Regiment of Foot
  Col. Richard Bassett's Regiment of Foot
  Col. Richard Donnell's Regiment of Foot

---

*   One line of thought puts them with Essex.
** Although it is not known which guns were drawn up in the grand battery, it is probable
    they were the heavier pieces of ordnance.

Centre: Col. Sir John Byron
First Line
Sgt Maj.-Gen. Thomas, Lord Wentworth's Commanded Muskets
Sgt Maj.-Gen. George Lisle's Commanded Muskets
Second Line
Part of Col. Sir John Byron's Brigade of Horse:
    Col. Sir John Byron's Regiment of Horse
    Col. Sir Thomas Aston's Regiment of Horse (George Boncle)
Col. Sir Nicholas Byron's Tertio (the Oxford Brigade)
    The King's Lifeguard Regiment of Foot (William Leighton)
    The Prince of Wales's Regiment of Foot (Sir Michael Woodhouse)
    Lord General, Earl of Forth's Regiment of Foot
    Col. St John, Lord Grandison's Regiment of Foot
    Col. Thomas Blagge's Regiment of Foot
    Col. Sir Lewis Dyve's Regiment of Foot
    Col. Sir Lewis Kirke's Regiment of Foot
    Col. Charles Gerard's Regiment of Foot (Edward Villiers)
    Col. Sir Henry Vaughan's Regiment of Foot
    Col. Conyers Darcy's Regiment of Foot (also Brigade commander?)
    Col. William Eure's Regiment of Foot (William Martin)
    Col. Thomas Pinchbeck's Regiment of Foot (Thomas Pinchbeck)
    Col. Henry, Lord Percy's Regiment of Foot (Henry Bard)

Left Wing: Prince Rupert of the Rhine
First Line
The following brigades are believed to have been formed:
    Col. Robert Dormer, Earl of Caernarvon's Brigade of Horse
    Prince Rupert's Brigade of Horse
    Lt-Gen. Henry, Lord Wilmot's Brigade of Horse
    Col. Charles Gerard's Brigade of Horse
    Sir John Byron's Brigade of Horse
The following regiments were present but their allocation is unknown. The grouping here is speculative:
    Col. Robert Dormer, Earl of Caernarvon's Regiment of Horse
    The Prince of Wales's Regiment of Horse (Thomas Daniel)
    Prince Maurice's Regiment of Horse (Robert Legge)
    Col. George Bridges, Lord Chandos' Regiment of Horse
    Col. James Compton, Earl of Northampton's Regiment of Horse
    Col. Sir Charles Lucas's Regiment of Horse
    Col. Sir Arthur Aston's Regiment of Horse
    Gen. Ralph, Lord Hopton's Regiment of Horse

The King's Lifeguard Regiment of Horse (Sir Bernard Stuart)
The Queen's Regiment of Horse (Lord Jermyn)
Prince Rupert's Lifeguard Regiment of Horse (Sir Richard Crane)
Prince Rupert's Regiment of Horse (Daniel O'Neale)
Lt-Gen. Henry, Lord Wilmot's Regiment of Horse
Col. George, Lord Digby's Regiment of Horse
Col. Henry, Lord Percy's Regiment of Horse
Col. Charles Howard, Lord Andover's Regiment of Horse

Col. Charles Gerard's Regiment of Horse
Col. Sir George Vaughan's Regiment of Horse
Col. Sir Thomas Tyldesley's Regiment of Horse

Col. Sir Samuel Sandy's Regiment of Horse
Col. Sir John Hurry's Regiment of Horse
Col. Sir Charles Lucas's Regiment of Horse
Col. Sir Thomas Morgan's Regiment of Horse

Regiments of Dragoons (unspecified attachment):
Prince Rupert's Regiment of Dragoons (Thomas Hooper)
Henry Washington's Regiment of Dragoons
Lord Wentworth's Regiment of Dragoons
Sir Robert Howard's Regiment of Dragoons

Second Line
Col. John Belasyse's Tertio:
Col. John Belasyse's Regiment of Foot (Sir Theophilus Gilbey)
Col. Sir Jacob Astley's Regiment of Foot (Toby Bowes)
Col. Richard Bolles' Regiment of Foot
Col. Sir Ralph Dutton's Regiment of Foot (Stephen Hawkins)
Col. John Owen's Regiment of Foot (Roger Burgess)
Col. Henry Lunsford's Regiment of Foot
Col. John Savage, Earl Rivers' Regiment of Foot (John Boys)

Col. Sir Gilbert Gerard's Tertio:
Col. Sir Gilbert Gerard's Regiment of Foot (Ratcliffe Gerard)
Col. Richard, Lord Molyneux's Regiment of Foot (Roger Nowell)
Col. Sir Edward Fitton's Regiment of Foot
Col. Sir Charles Lloyd's Regiment of Foot
Col. Sir Edward Stradling's Regiment of Foot (John Stradling)
Col. Anthony Thelwell's Regiment of Foot
Col. Sir Thomas Tyldesley's Regiment of Foot (Hugh Anderton)

Col. Sir Thomas Blackwell's Regiment of Foot
Col. Richard Herbert's Regiment of Foot (Arthur Blayney)

Unlisted units thought also to have been at Newbury I:
Col. William Eure's Regiment of Horse

Ordnance: Gen. of the Ordnance Col. Henry, Lord Percy
The Field Battery of Artillery*
Col. Henry, Lord Percy's Company of Firelocks

The royal train consisted of:

Heavy	Medium	Light
2 demi-cannons	5 6-pdrs	2 minions
2 culverins	I saker	4 3-pdrs
2 12-pdrs		2 bases

According to period practice, the lighter guns were probably spread along the line to accompany the Foot tertios.

Newbury II   ORDER OF BATTLE   PARLIAMENTARIAN

West Wing: General of the Southern Association Sir William Waller
Lieutenant General Sir Arthur Haselrig
Sergeant Major-General of Foot Philip Skippon
Lieutenant General of the Horse Sir William Balfour
Quartermaster General John Dalbier
Quartermaster General of Foot Jeremy Baines
Scoutmaster General James Pitsom

The Right: Lt-Gen. William Balfour
Lt-Gen. William Balfour's Brigade of Horse from Essex's Army:
    Earl of Essex's Lifeguard Troop of Horse
    Earl of Essex's Regiment of Horse
    Lt-Gen. Sir William Balfour's Regiment of Horse (Maj. William Balfour)
    QM Gen. John Dalbier's Regiment of Horse
    Com.-Gen. Hans Behre's Regiment of Horse (Samuel Bosa)
    Lt-Gen. Sir Philip Stapleton's Regiment of Horse

* Although it is not known which guns were drawn up in the grand battery, it is probable they were the six heavier pieces of ordnance plus two of the bigger mediums.

Col. Edmund Harvey's Regiment of Horse
Col. James Sheffield's Regiment of Horse
Col. Sir Robert Pye's Regiment of Horse
Lt-Gen. Sir Philip Stapleton's Troop of Dragoons
Lt-Gen. Sir Arthur Haselrig's Brigade of Horse from Waller's Army:
  Gen. Sir William Waller's Regiment of Horse
  Lt-Gen. Sir Arthur Haselrig's Regiment of Horse (John Okey?)
  Col. John Fitzjames' Regiment of Horse
  Col. John Fiennes' Regiment of Horse
Lt-Gen. John Middleton's Brigade of Horse from Waller's Army:
  Lt-Gen. John Middleton's Regiment of Horse
  Col. Edward Cooke's Regiment of Horse
  Gen. Sir William Waller's Regiment of Dragoons

The Centre: Sgt Maj.-Gen. Philip Skippon

Lt-Col. Butler:
  Earl of Essex's Regiment of Foot
Col. Henry Barclay's Brigade of Foot from Essex's Army:
  Sgt Maj.-Gen. Philip Skippon's Regiment of Foot
  Lord Robartes' Regiment of Foot (William Hunter)
  Col. Henry Barclay's Regiment of Foot
Col. Edward Aldrich's Brigade of Foot from Essex's Army:
  Col. Edward Aldrich's Regiment of Foot (W. Lloyd)
  Col. Adam Cunningham's Regiment of Foot (Richard Fortescue)
  Col. William Davies's Regiment of Foot
  Col. Thomas Tyrell's Regiment of Foot (Richard Ingoldsby)
Sir James Harrington's London Brigade of Foot:
  The Red Regiment of the City Trained Bands
  The Blue Regiment of the City Trained Bands
  The Red Regiment of the Westminster Trained Bands
  The Yellow Regiment of the Tower Hamlets Auxiliaries

The Left: Lt-Gen. Oliver Cromwell

Lt-Gen. Oliver Cromwell's Brigade of Horse from Manchester's Army:
  Lt-Gen. Oliver Cromwell's Regiment of Horse (Edward Whalley)
  Col. Bartholomew Vermuyden's Regiment of Horse

East Wing: General of the Eastern Association Edward Montagu, Earl of Manchester

Lieutenant General of Horse Edmund Ludlow
Sergeant Major-General of Foot Lawrence Crawford
Lieutenant General of Artillery Thomas Hammond

Staff Colonel John Birch
Commissary General Jonas Vandrusques
Scoutmaster General Leon Wason

The Horse
Lt-Gen. Edmund Ludlow's Brigade of Horse:
    Lt-Gen. Edmund Ludlow's Regiment of Horse (Wansey)
    Col. Richard Norton's Regiment of Horse
Unknown Brigade of Horse:
    Earl of Manchester's Regiment of Horse (Algernon Sidney)
    Col. Charles Fleetwood's Regiment of Horse
    Earl of Manchester's Regiment of Dragoons (John Lilburne)
Maj.-Gen. Brown's London Brigade of Horse:
    Maj.-Gen. Brown's Regiment of Horse
    Col. Richard Mainwaring's Regiment of Horse
    Col. William Underwood's Regiment of Horse

The Foot: Sgt Maj.-Gen. Lawrence Crawford
Brigade of Foot:
    Earl of Manchester's Regiment of Foot (Clifton)
Brigade of Foot:
    Sgt Maj.-Gen. Lawrence Crawford's Regiment of Foot (William Hamilton)
    Col. Sir Miles Hobart's Regiment of Foot
Sgt Maj.-Gen. Lawrence Crawford's Brigade of Foot:
    Col. Edward Montagu's Regiment of Foot
    Col. John Pickering's Regiment of Foot
    Col. Francis Russell's Regiment of Foot
Brigade of Foot:
    Col. Sir Thomas Hoogan's Regiment of Foot
    Col. Thomas Rainsborough's Regiment of Foot
    Col. Valentine Walton's Regiment of Foot

Although the Eastern Association had seriously decreased in size after Marston Moor, many regiments in Manchester's army were reinforced or freshly recruited and were substantially larger than those which had taken part in Essex's and Waller's campaigns, hence the fewer regiments in each brigade. Some secondary sources include regiments from Waller's Foot and the London Auxiliaries. Primary sources are uncited so the presence of both brigades is very doubtful.

Sgt Maj.-Gen. James Holborne's Brigade of Foot from Waller's Army:
    Col. Thomas Carre's Regiment of Foot

Sgt Maj.-Gen. James Holborne's/Haselrig's Regiment of Foot
Col. William Jephson's Regiment of Foot
Col. Samuel Jones's Regiment of Foot
Maj.-Gen. Brown's London Brigade of Foot:*
  The Red Regiment of the City of London Auxiliaries (Harsnet)
  The Blue Regiment of the City of London Auxiliaries (Pindar)
  The White Regiment of the City of London Auxiliaries (Shepherd)

Newbury II   ORDER OF BATTLE   ROYALIST

Commander in Chief Charles Stuart, King of England

Lord General Patrick Ruthven, Earl of Brentford
Lieutenant General of Horse George, Lord Goring
Sergeant Major-General of Foot Jacob, Lord Astley
General of Artillery Ralph, Lord Hopton
Quartermaster and Engineer General Charles Lloyd

Right Wing: Jacob, Lord Astley

Colonel Sir George Lisle's Tertio (including the Reading Brigade):
  Col. Sir George Lisle's Regiment of Foot
  Col. Sir Thomas Blackwell's Regiment of Foot
  Col. William Eure's Regiment of Foot (Francis Martin)
  Col. Theophilus Gilbey's Regiment of Foot
  Col. Charles Lloyd's Regiment of Foot
  Col. John Owen's Regiment of Foot
  Col. John Stradling's Regiment of Foot
  Col. Anthony Thelwell's Regiment of Foot
  Col. Sir Henry Vaughan's Regiment of Foot
Col. Sir Bernard Astley's Tertio:
  Col. Sir Allan Apsley's Regiment of Foot
  Col. Sir Bernard Astley's Regiment of Foot
  Col. Matthew Appleyard's Regiment of Foot
  Col. Sir William Courtney's Regiment of Foot
  Col. Francis Cooke's Regiment of Foot
  Gen. Ralph, Lord Hopton's Regiment of Foot
  Col. Sir John Paulet's Regiment of Foot
  Col. Sir Edward Rodney's Regiment of Foot
  Col. Henry Shelley's Regiment of Foot

---

* If these additional London regiments were present, it would explain the buff-coats stripped
  from the dead of the diversionary attack and support Money's claim that there were
  Londoners with both Waller and Manchester.

Col. Walter Slingsby's Regiment of Foot
Col. John Talbot's Regiment of Foot
Sir John Browne's temporary Brigade of Horse from Wentworth's:
    The Prince of Wales's Regiment of Horse
    Prince Rupert's Dragoons (Sir Thomas Hooper)

Centre: His Majesty King Charles I
Col. Thomas Blagge's Tertio:
    The King's Lifeguard of Foot
    Lord Gen. Ruthven's Regiment of Foot
    Gen. Jacob, Lord Astley's Regiment of Foot
    Col. Sir Henry Bard's Regiment of Foot
    Col. Sir James Pennyman's Regiment of Foot
    Col. Henry, Lord Percy's Regiment of Foot (William Murray)
    Col. Thomas Blagge's Regiment of Foot (detachment under Sir William Lower)

Centre Horse: General of Horse, George, Lord Goring
Thomas Wentworth, Earl of Cleveland's Brigade of Horse:
    Earl of Cleveland's Regiment of Horse
    Col. Sir Nicholas Crispe's Regiment of Horse
    Col. Dutton Fleetwood's Regiment of Horse
    Col. James Hamilton's Regiment of Horse
    Col. Richard Thornhill's Regiment of Horse
    Col. Thomas Culpepper's Regiment of Horse
Lord Wentworth's Brigade of Horse:
    The Queen's Regiment of Horse (Sir John Cansfield)
    Col. Richard Neville's Regiment of Horse
    Col. Sir William Boteler's Regiment of Horse?
Unbrigaded Regiment of Horse:
    The King's Lifeguard of Horse (Lord Bernard Stuart)
Col. Sir Humphrey Bennet's Brigade of Horse:
    Col. Sir Humphrey Bennet's Regiment of Horse
    Col. Sir George Vaughan's Regiment of Horse
    Col. Sir Edward Waldegrave's Regiment of Horse
    Col. Andrew Lyndsay's Regiment of Horse
Col. Thomas Howard's Brigade of Horse (possibly now under Hopton?):
    Lord Gen. Ruthven's Regiment of Horse
    Prince Maurice's Regiment of Horse
    Col. Gerard Crocker's Regiment of Horse
    Col. Thomas Howard's Regiment of Horse (Robert Howard)
    Col. Thomas Weston's Regiment of Horse

Col. Sir Arthur Slingsby's Regiment of Horse
Unknown allocation:
    Gen. Ralph, Lord Hopton's Regiment of Horse
    Marquis of Hertford's Regiment of Horse
    Col. Sir Edward Ford's Regiment of Horse
    Col. George Custer and Col. Allan Apsley's combined Regiment of Horse
    Col. Edward Pierce's Regiment of Horse

Donnington Castle: Sir John Boys
Col. Earl Rivers' Regiment of Foot
Col. Sir John Boys' Troop of Horse

Left Wing: Prince Maurice of the Palatinate
Sgt Maj.-Gen. Sir Thomas Basset's Tertio:
    Sgt Maj.-Gen. Sir Thomas Basset's Regiment of Foot
    Col. Sir John Grenville's Regiment of Foot
    Col. Thomas St Aubyn's Regiment of Foot
    Col. William Godolphin's Regiment of Foot
Col. Sir Edward Cary's Brigade of Foot:
    Prince Maurice's Regiment of Foot (Philip Champernon)*
    Lt-Gen. John Digby's Regiment of Foot
    Col. Sir Edward Cary's Regiment of Foot
    Col. Sir John/Richard Arundell's Regiment of Foot
    Col. Sir Edmund Fortescue's Regiment of Foot
    Col. Sir John Ackland's Regiment of Foot
    Col. Richard Vivian's Regiment of Foot
    Col. Thomas Hele's Regiment of Foot
    Col. Bullen Reyne's Regiment of Foot
Also noted by secondary sources but allocation unknown:
    Col. Joseph Bamfield's Regiment of Foot
    Col. Piers Edgecombe's Regiment of Foot
    Col. Thomas Pigot's Regiment of Foot
    Col. John Stocker's Regiment of Foot
    Col. Joseph Wagstaffe's Regiment of Foot
Unbrigaded Regiment of Foot from Blagge's Tertio:
    James, Duke of York's Regiment of Foot (William St Leger)
Lt-Gen. John Digby's Brigade of Horse:**

---

* Whether Champernon had his own regiment or commanded Prince Maurice's is unknown.
** Some evidence suggests Digby's command was divided into two brigades under Sir Thomas Aston and Sir Francis Doddington but their composition is unknown.

Prince Maurice's Regiment of Horse
Col. Sir Thomas Basset's Regiment of Horse
Col. Sir Henry Cary's Regiment of Horse
Col. Sir Edward Stawell's Regiment of Horse
Col. Sir Francis Doddington's Regiment of Horse
Col. Piers Edgecombe's Regiment of Horse
Col. Marcus Trevor's Regiment of Horse

Boxford: Sir John Douglas
Unknown Regiment of Foot
Unknown Regiment of Horse

The Royalist regiments were small compared to the Parliamentarian ones.

Chapter Seven

SUMMARY

Deciding who won and who lost a battle is sometimes achieved by comparing the casualties of both sides. However, coming to an understanding of the numbers of killed and wounded on each side as a result of both battles of Newbury is not easy. Contemporary claims were either exaggerated or minimised according to propaganda demands and later estimates have been based upon successive authors' discoveries and predilections. The table below sets out the various claims, although I return to my own original estimate of about 1,200 per side for Newbury I and about half that per side for Newbury II. The lists of casualties below have been gleaned from several sources to show just how varied the reporting can be.

NEWBURY I

Source estimating losses	Parliament	Royalist
Heath's Chronicle	6,000	5,000
Mon. de Larrey	4,000	4,000
Oldmixon	500	2,000
Money	5,000	5,000
Barratt	1,200	1,300

Royalists Killed:

The Earl of Caernarvon
Lucius Carey, Lord Falkland
Sir Anthony Mansel
Col. Poole
Col. Richard Platt
Col. Wheatley
Col. Slingsby

The Earl of Sunderland
The Hon. Henry Bertie
Col. Joseph Constable
Col. Murray
Col. Pinchbeck
Col. Eure
Col. Thomas Morgan

Col. Stroud
Capt. William Symcocks
Capt. Thomas Singleton
Capt. Bernard Brocas
Lt George Collingwood
Other officers (ranks unknown):
Algernon Simes

Capt. Robert Molineux
Capt. Francis Bartis
Capt. Francis Clifton
Lt Henry Butler
Lt William Culcheth

Royalist Wounded:
The Earl of Carlisle
Lord Andover
The Hon. Edward Sackville
Sir John Russell
Col. George Lisle
Col. Thomas Dalton
Col. Ivers
Col. Edward Villiers
Col. Spencer
Mr Progers

The Earl of Peterborough
Lord Chandos
Sir Charles Lucas
Sir Edward Waldegrave
Col. Fielding
Col. Gerard
Col. D'Arcy
Col. Howard
Capt. Thurston Andrews
George Porter

Parliament Killed:
Col. Davies
Col. Tucker
Col. Greaves
Capt. Hunt
Capt. Talbot
Capt. Massey
Capt. Mosse
Capt. Juxon

Col. Bamfield
Col. Mainwaring
Col. White
Capt. Ware
Capt. St Barbe
Capt. Bolton
Capt. Stoning
Capt. Willet

Parliament Wounded:
QM Gen. John Dalbier
Col. Dalbier
Capt. Fleetwood
Cornet D'Oyley

Com. Gen. Copley
Capt. Hammond
Capt. Charles Pym

Sir Henry Anderson wrote, 'The sight of so many brought to Oxford, some dead, some wounded, since the battle, would make every true English heart bleed.'

NEWBURY II

Source estimating losses	Parliament	Royalist
Sir Edward Walker	—	588
Manley	2,500	5,000
Whitelock	—	200
Money	—	—
Clarendon	1,000	500

Royalist Killed:

Sir William St Leger
Lt-Col. Houghton
Lt-Col. Jones
Maj. Knyvett
Capt. Catelyn
Capt. Philpot
Mr Barksdale

Lt-Col. Leke
Lt-Col. Topping
Maj. Trevellian
Capt. Whittingham
Capt. Wolfall
Capt. Mildmay

Royalist Wounded:

Patrick Ruthven, Earl of Brentford
Sir John Grenville
Sir Edward Waldegrave
Maj. Alford
Lt George Hume

Sir John Campsfield
Lt-Col. Richard Page
Capt. Wells
Mr Stephen Knight

Parliament Killed:

Col. Gawler
Lt-Col. White
Charles D'Oyley

Lt-Col. Knight
Capt. Willet

Parliament Wounded:

Col. Norton
Col. Lloyd

Col. Berkley
Lt George Haines

From the casualties we might deduce that honours were 'about equal' in both battles but we must also consider the tactical and strategic implications.

These were two very different tactical battles. Newbury I was an example of one side having a clear plan while the other did not, and on the day the latter only responded to what their opponents did. The Royalists found themselves in a similar position to the British at Quatre Bras: they had the strategic advantage but had relinquished the tactical initiative and consequently had to keep deploying troops to meet attacks as they developed. Wellington likened that prelude to Waterloo as an engagement in which he had to keep knotting a rope, and perhaps Charles and Rupert felt the same as first Essex advanced, then Skippon and Robartes, which in turn obliged them to attack or admit campaign defeat. Newbury II was a much simpler affair. The King's forces had established a defensive perimeter and dug in, while the Parliamentarians effected a pincer-like movement, with Manchester launching two attacks in the east and Waller striking hard from the west. An attack on prepared positions has been likened to waves breaking on a seawall; it is usually a dramatic stalemate – and so it was at Newbury, despite one section of 'wall' giving way.

Strategically the two battles may have been occasioned by the town's geographical location at the junction of the major roads of central southern England and its bridge over a principal waterway, the Kennet, but Newbury I was very much a Parliamentarian victory, as the King failed to prevent Essex from returning to his depot in London. Newbury II is rather more complicated, for although the Royalists quit the field, Manchester and Waller failed to follow up and destroy them, enabling them to regroup and return later with reinforcements. Strategically this was a more of a draw in the short term, with Parliament winning the initial strategic advantage then throwing it away.

However, with hindsight we can see that the two battles of Newbury had very different long-term strategic outcomes. Indeed, Newbury I has been called 'the turning-point' of the First Civil War. For the Royalists the Gloucester and Newbury campaign of 1643, despite a number of well-fought actions and much heroic gallantry, had been a woeful chronicle of misleading advice, lost opportunities and poor decisions culminating in a sorry return to Oxford. Before Newbury I the Royalists had held the initiative, and successes such as Braddock Down in January, Hopton Heath and Seacroft Moor in March, Ripple Field in April, Stratton in May, Chalgrove and Adwalton Moor in June, plus Roundway Down, the taking of Bristol and the arrival of the Queen's convoy in July had all given rise to a feeling that overall victory for their cause was certain. Newbury I was a reversal of this series of successes for the King and his Army of Oxford had experienced bitter failure. The Parliamentarians, in contrast, could breathe a sigh of relief. Not only had their Lord General proved himself an able commander but their army had proved itself equal to that of the Royalists. The King's run of victories had been interrupted, the untested London regiments had shown themselves capable of fighting and the regular regiments had garnered renewed morale and determination. The capital was safely garrisoned and their military base was secure, which meant financial and mercantile business could continue undisturbed; their sinews of war were strong and protected. With the advantage of hindsight we can observe that Newbury I saw the end of Royalist dominance and the beginning of the rise of Parliamentarian success.

The major result of Newbury II was not one that can be measured in tactical or even strategic terms. It was not so much a Churchillian 'punctuation mark of history', but the opening of a new chapter in the war.

The post-battle recriminations among the Parliamentarian commanders, especially between Manchester and Cromwell, descended into acrimonious accusations and counter-attacks, which eventually manifested themselves as formal complaints put before the Committee of Both Kingdoms and the House. It was obvious that despite their successes there was still a considerable problem. Earlier Waller had written of his soldiers, 'these men will never go through with your service, and till you have an army merely your own that you may command, it is in a manner impossible to do anything of importance'. Cromwell too had reflected upon this subject to Hampden:

> How can we be otherwise than beaten? Your troops are old, decayed serving men and tapsters and such kind of fellows; and they are gentlemen's sons, younger sons, and persons of quality; but I will remedy that. I will raise men who will have the fear of God before their eyes and will bring some conscience to what they do, and I promise you they shall not be beaten.

Newbury II made Cromwell even more determined to take up this torch. The disparity of quality between the two armies became almost a fixation with him; it was certainly one of the driving forces behind many of his subsequent speeches and letters. His single-minded pursuit of this doctrine propelled him ever further up the military and political ladders, and resulted, first and foremost, in the Self-Denying Ordinance, by which most politicians were obliged to relinquish their military commissions. There were four exceptions, including Cromwell himself. Secondly, it gave rise to the formation of the New Model Army: Parliament's new professional and independent army trained and commanded by Sir Thomas Fairfax with Cromwell as his Lieutenant General of Horse. The story of the New Model Army is well known, and through its continuing success and his own abilities both in the field and in the House Cromwell achieved even greater power and influence, eventually becoming Lord General of all Parliament's armies and finally Lord Protector of England.

Chapter Eight

TOURING THE BATTLEFIELDS

Newbury is in west Berkshire, near the border with Wiltshire. It lies on the junction of the A4 and A34, a couple of miles south of the M4 (junction 13). It is a growing town and, like many of its ilk, it is gradually encroaching on to the surrounding countryside. Unfortunately for military historians, both battles of Newbury were fought close to the town and much of the ground over which they were fought has already been or soon will be sold to developers and thus lost for ever.

Two things should be considered before contemplating a tour of the battlefields. The first is Health and Safety. Of prime importance, this aspect of battlefield walking or touring should be kept in mind at all times. Whether walking or driving along country lanes, or even strolling through fields, you should familiarise yourself with any dangers involved and take every reasonable step to negate possible risk to yourself or your companions. This is not the nanny state but common sense. Cows in pastures are not always placid, and trips, slips and falls easily occur. Some unthinking drivers do go too fast and some of the lanes on both Newburys do have blind corners. Anyone intending to conduct groups around any battlefield should read the relevant H&S guidelines and carry a mobile phone.

The second thing to keep in mind is that the land you are crossing belongs to somebody, no matter how strong your Leveller convictions and sense of the Right to Roam. You must ensure you do no damage and you must observe the Country Code. Access to both battlefields is reasonable, although some viewpoints can be tricky. Always ask permission to enter private property or to photograph a feature. Several major and minor roads run across the battlefields, and while some seem to follow the line of old country lanes, others have been put in fairly recently and a few have been straightened (notably the Enborne Road). There are plenty of public footpaths, many of which allow battlefield walkers access. I have wandered over both fields many times but I have yet to encounter anyone from the 'Get off my land' brigade, except at the school, despite the unfriendly notices that abound near the more upmarket properties!

It is also worth considering the light. Both battles were fought in the autumn when the nights were drawing in and both ended because of failing daylight. This is critical with Newbury II as calculations using the New Style Calendar effectively shift the date to the modern 6 November in terms of sunlight hours. Dawn is around 7.00am and Richard Holmes states sunset was at 4.26pm, with the moon in its first quarter and setting shortly after midnight. In other words, it got dark early and the moon didn't give much light either. If Manchester began his major attack at 4.00pm they only had 26 minutes of daylight to storm Shaw House and the village before the gloom set in. For those who like to visit battlefields on anniversaries, it might be wise to start as early as possible.

The battlefield of Newbury I has changed since 1643 owing to the varying demands of housing, farming and transport. This process started in the eighteenth century when the Kennet and Avon Canal was cut through the northern sector of the battlefield, and more recently the north-east sector where the Royalist army camped and arrayed has succumbed to housing estates, light industrial factories, new roads and a major by-pass. Luckily, the majority of the ground where much of the fighting probably took place is still farmland, although areas of land once left fallow have recently been given over to crops. Added to that, many of the hedges have been grubbed out to increase profitability and field-bordering trees have grown up where

NEWBURY I

Campaign:	Essex's Gloucester Campaign
War period:	First Civil War
Outcome:	Indecisive Parliamentarian victory
County:	West Berkshire
Place:	Newbury/Enbourne
Terrain:	Enclosed fields, commons and copses
Date:	20 September 1643
Start:	7:00am
Duration:	12 hours
Armies:	Parliament: Earl of Essex and Philip Skippon
	Royalist: King Charles I and Prince Rupert
Numbers:	About 15,000 per side
Losses:	About 1,200 per side
OS Explorer map:	158
Grid Reference:	43–45:63–68

once scrubland bushes held sway, but essentially most of the crucial areas of action have escaped drastic alteration. At the time of writing (2007) two portions of Wash Common remain reasonably untouched, the first to the west and south of Wash Common Farm, despite a cricket club and an expensive housing project, and the second to the south of Monkey Lane, where the expanse of scrub is beginning to be nibbled at by the relocated college and Vodaphone. Nevertheless, although the area is still largely countryside, I doubt that either Essex or Rupert would recognise their battlefield today. It is not easy, however, to translate the events of 20 September 1643 on to a modern rural landscape. We are fortunate that the landscape itself has not changed much despite the eyesore earthworks of the Newbury A34 by-pass that thunders through the Parliamentarian position.

Although it was one of the major battles of the First Civil War, Newbury I is still subject to controversy about its exact location, especially in the southern sector. We know approximately where the various actions that constitute the battle took place but we cannot yet be precise. Hence the battle story and guided tour given here are based on an interpretation that has been gleaned from both primary and secondary sources and subjected to the application of the Three Perspectives of Battlefield Interpretation. Even so, this, and any other version found in past, current or even future publications, will remain 'unproven' until a thorough, detailed examination of the ground and its archaeology is undertaken.

These tour notes are written for those who prefer to drive around big battlefields. Of course others prefer to walk, as I do, but if visitors have limited time and wish to see the whole battlefield in one day, or even try to see both battles, then travelling by car between stands becomes essential. However, battles are not restricted to roads, despite many battles being interpreted by car-bound authors, and events and locations being made to fit the easy access. If you are a confirmed battlefield walker, please use OS Explorer 158 to plot your own route between stands and feel free to visit them in the order which suits you best.

To find Newbury I

Leave the M4 at Junction 13 and head south on the A34 dual carriageway. Ignore the signpost for Newbury (A339), and stay on the A34 (ring road) heading for Winchester and Southampton, which loops to the west of the town. At the first junction, signposted to Hungerford and Newbury (A4), slip off to the left. At the mini-roundabout take the second exit, effectively turning right, towards Hungerford. Just after the bridge over the dual carriageway park on the side of the road. Normally the A4 is a fairly quiet road but at peak times there are large lorries and heavy traffic so it would probably be wise to leave your hazard lights on. Get out of the car and look south. This is Stand One of the tour and before you is the expanse of the northern and central sectors of the battlefield of Newbury I.

A battlefield tour for the First Battle of Newbury
STAND ONE: The General Picture

The view is rather spectacular but bear in mind that in 1643 the battlefield was covered with far more enclosures and hedges, although fewer trees. The easiest landmark to distinguish is the modern water tower breaking the skyline over to the left; this resembles a square church tower at a distance. This water tower roughly marks the centre of the Royalist position and is next to the Falkland Recreation Ground, where the Royalist main battery was deployed. The line of trees falling away to the left indicates the Royalist deployment line. Looking along the skyline to the right you should be able to make out the rising ground of Round Hill, although that too is now rather overgrown with trees.

With binoculars you should be able to see some houses to the east on the west-facing slope where Byron deployed his front line, and slightly to the right you will see the field east of Round Hill where Byron's men fought

The northern sector of Newbury I.

136

The Falkland Monument is a convenient landmark for directions, but is of limited use for battlefield interpretation. In the background is another famous landmark, the Gun Inn.

Skippon's. Below that hill and nearer to you is Skinner's Green, where the Parliamentarian Reserve was positioned, while to the east of the A34 (and a lot nearer to you) are the fields over which the Parliamentarian Left advanced. If you keep watching that area you might see a vehicle drive along the Newbury–Enborne road, which runs from right to left across the mid-ground. Vavasour's Royalist and Robartes' Parliamentarian brigades were in the fields on either side of it, while some of Middleton's Horse were even nearer your standpoint, towards the tree-line that follows the banks of the River Kennet. The A34 dual carriageway roughly follows the Parliamentarian line. To the right of the dual carriageway is Crockham Heath, and the ground rises to Enborne and Craven Hills where Essex had his camp and his baggage. The Royalist camp was over the horizon to the left, while the Royalist baggage was back in Newbury.

To see the southern sector of the battlefield you need to drive through Newbury. More adventurous visitors may care to explore the rear of Essex's position by heading for Hungerford and turning first left for a tour of the country lanes via Marsh Benham, Hamstead Marshall and Enborne, but the more direct route heads towards Newbury via the mini-roundabouts on the A4. This route takes you through Speen, which features in the story of Newbury II. Please note that the 30mph limit is strictly enforced by cameras. Stay on the A4 until you join the inner ring road (A339) and then follow signs for the town centre and A339. You will cross both the River Kennet and the Kennet and Avon Canal.

At the roundabout, currently next to Burger King, turn right for Andover along St John's Road. At the next roundabout take the A343 for Andover, Enborne and Wash Common. You will pass St Bartholomew's School on your right, and then climb a long hill. This is Wash Lane and the site of the royal camp, and the road names to either side recall several heroes of the battle. Again please note that there are speed cameras in the trees. The ground rises to the edge of Wash Common and a 'double roundabout' crossroads. This is the centre of the Royalist line, marked by the Falkland Monument. Turn right into Essex Street, with the obelisk on your left. If you wish to visit the monument, turn right immediately into the car park of a small shopping precinct.

About 200m along Essex Street you will see a brick building on the right

This farmhouse, now divided into two residences and 'modernised', was one of only two buildings known to have stood on Wash Common during the battle. It was here that the body of Lord Falkland was brought.

on the corner of a side road called Falkland Garth. Despite the 1926 plaque on the porch, this is the much-altered farmhouse to which Falkland's body was first taken. Some historians have argued that it must have been a dressing station and that there may have been some hope of saving his life, but although there may well have been designated places for the care of the wounded, this story has no foundation.

After another 100m turn right into Elizabeth Avenue and follow the road as it winds down through a 1950s housing estate. The road drops into the valley across which Byron's men advanced in order to assault Fortescue's and Skippon's men in the enclosures in front of Round Hill. The slopes on the right witnessed Byron's advance and those on the left are where they attacked. The gradient flattens out as the road name changes to Valley Road. At the T-junction turn left along Fifth Road and, ignoring the left bend up Oken Grove, keep going until the tarmac runs out. Stop and park at the end of the short stretch of unmade road. You will see a sign indicating this point as a footpath crossroads.

STAND TWO: Vavasour's Left
Ahead is a track that takes you directly west towards Skinner's Green and the place where the Blue Auxiliaries came to plug the gap between Skippon and Robartes. If you have time a walk down this track, which Money calls 'the Old Enborne Road', is rewarding. You will come to a wooded cross-roads with fine views across the fields up to Round Hill. There is also a lane to your right that leads northwards to the Enborne road. This overgrown lane has been suggested as one which was disputed by the commanded muskets of Vavasour and Robartes at both the beginning and the end of the action, and the fields west of it as one of the major fighting areas for the troops on this flank. If you follow this lane to the Enborne road you will emerge near Guyer's Lane, now labelled 'Footpath Only', which leads over a canal bridge to the Kennet and is where Vavasour held Robartes' counter-attack late in the day.

Remember these fields are not the same size as they were in 1643; many enclosure hedges have been torn out and until a period field study is published we can only guess at the location of the hedges that were contested on the day, although Google Earth does give some indication. However, it is easy to see that the land is flat and had trees not grown up over the years the view of the whole sector would have been good. Vavasour and Robartes would have been able to see any reinforcements being sent to either side, and any redeployment of enemy troops could be easily countered. In addition, the flat ground meant that fields of fire for the light guns which accompanied the Foot were also unhindered, apart from the hedgerows.

The fields south of the Enborne road and possibly the hedge where Robartes' forlorn hope first met Vavasour's attack and where his final counter-attack took place.

Go back to the car. Retrace your route up Valley Road and turn right into Garforth Crescent. Drive on a little way past Rankin Junior School, round the bend on to flatter ground where it is easier to park. Take the footpath just to the south of the school which leads up a short, steep slope to the open field.

STAND THREE: Wentworth's Track
Coming down the slope towards you at the side of the field is what is thought to be the track down which Wentworth's and Lisle's commanded muskets moved to reinforce the Right. It was a footpath long before the field was cultivated and walkers had to keep off the crops. If you walk southwards up this track you will notice it is actually on a slight reverse slope and so would allow concealed movement from most of the battlefield to the west.

Walk westward along the field's bottom edge to the end of the tree-line. Round Hill is silhouetted against the skyline on your left. Directly to the

The view from the north up Round Hill. The trees indicate its crest, while the water-tower on the left gives the rough position of the royal guns. Springate's advance on Byron's troops, who occupied the land between the two features, was over the fields in the foreground.

west is the ground Springates' Regiment of Foot wheeled across so as to bring their fire to bear upon the flank of Byron's attack. Evidence suggests that their left flank, which would have been left dangerously exposed to enemy fire, was in fact covered by a hedge, which no doubt they would have lined with files of musketeers while they performed this wheeling manoeuvre. Retrace your steps back to the car.

Leave Garforth Crescent and turn right up Elizabeth Way to the top of the hill (you will pass a small Costcutters supermarket on the left which might be handy for refreshments). At the junction with Essex Street turn right and go west for about 100m, then turn left into Battle Road. At the end of the road, about 100m, there is a small rectangular car park next to the Falkland Recreation Ground, where you can leave the car while you explore the Royalist position on foot. This car park is locked during the evening and there is some confusion about the time – do check if in doubt. If there is a problem you can always park in Battle Road or Stuart Road. There is a brick-built public toilet but I have never found it unlocked. One local resident told me that this park is rather unsavoury after dark.

STAND FOUR: The Royalist Grand Battery

Walk out into the centre of the park. This is where the major Royalist gun battery was set up on a diagonal north-east–south-west line, with its right pointing north-east towards the Falkland Monument. There is a plaque commemorating the events of the battle on the southern mound. Deployed after coming up Monkey Lane, there were supposedly eight large pieces here, possibly two demi-cannon, two culverins, two 12-pdrs and two other heavy guns. Some sources state the mound is part of a work hastily thrown up the night before the battle ready to receive the guns, while others say it is an ancient tumulus. The guns were set on an angle so that their arc of fire could cover both the forward crest in the direction of the water tower and tumuli, and Round Hill, across Battle Road. It's not much of a trail-spike shift of angle, even for a whole battery.

The train necessary to bring up and keep these guns in action would be kept at a distance behind the line, most likely utilising the track that is now Andover Road. This might have served as the powder and ball field replenishment area for the whole army as its Reserve was back in Newbury on the other side of the Kennet in what is now Victoria Park – an extraordinary distance to bring up ammunition.

The commemoration stone on the site of the royal battery; authorities differ on when the mound on which it sits was thrown up.

Now walk back to Battle Road and go north to Essex Street. (If you prefer to drive, turn left out of Battle Road and park in a pull-in on the right some 50m to the west). Opposite the end of Battle Road there is an almost hidden footpath to the left of Boundary Cottage. It is narrow and often overgrown, but follow it until a gap in the undergrowth on the left allows you access into the field. This has a perimeter track running left and right. Turn right and follow the edge of the field along the top of the western escarpment. If you follow it down the hill you will reach Stand Three.

STAND FIVE: Skippon's Hedges
Here, on the eastern edge of the enclosures, was the first hedge that Skippon lined, and the first obstacle Byron's men had to take from Fortescue's to establish their foothold on the plateau. The Parliamentarian commanded musketeers could easily have ranged across the valley and shot at Wentworth's and Lisle's men as they descended the far slopes and again as they toiled up the one in front of you. Only when the Royalists had cleared the Parliamentarians from this vantage point could the remainder of Byron's Foot make the ascent. Looking at the steepness of the slope one has to question the viability of getting Horse up it. It is likely that Byron's mounted troops came down Essex Street and then turned north up this track and deployed in the field to the west before making their attack. There is a path directly west, across the field, but it is not signposted as a public right of way.

Retrace your steps to the entrance gap but continue past it, following the pathway as it curves to the right. You will come to another track leading north, and to the south there is a metal gateway leading on to Essex Street. This was once a hedged lane and although both hedges have been grubbed out, traces of them can still be discerned, notably three large bushes set at intervals along the left-hand side of the track. Although now a tractor way, on Rocque's map this was a lane leading down to the Enborne road, and during the battle it would have been a major obstacle. This is substantiated by a study of the satellite picture available on Google Earth. Furthermore, this lane is in an appropriate position to fit both the contemporary accounts and local historian Money's interpretation as Darke Lane. As a double-hedged lane it would have been much harder to take than the previous one, but it must have had access gaps, probably 'gated' in the local fashion of wedging a stout branch or two across the gap, rammed into the hedge on either side. Walk down the track until you reach a point midway between the first and second of the three bushes, then look east.

On this land was the little enclosure which Nicholas Byron's Tertio fought so hard to take, especially Colonel Charles Gerard's Regiment of Foot. Somewhere in this field they lost 16 officers, 7 NCOs and 79 soldiers.

Byron's Enclosure. Over this small field Byron advanced on the fateful Darke Lane; this place cost him his horse and Falkland his life.

Imagine three regiments advancing from the hedge opposite across this space under close-range musket fire, and being forced back again after failing to get over the hedge immediately in front of you. Somewhere along here too was the dangerous gap through which Byron drove his own mount, only to have it shot from under him. He was followed by Lord Falkland, who paid with his life for this tiny bridgehead through the obstacle and died in this lane, in the process buying enough time for others to widen the gap. Once they were in the lane, they could advance both up and down the lane cutting into the flanks of the musketeers manning it. If you turn round and face west you will see their next objective – yet another hedge.

This one was Byron's undoing, as not only had the Parliamentarians got behind it but they also had two small guns loaded with case-shot hidden in it! This was a hedge too far. The hedges in this area are trimmed today but in the 1600s they were allowed to grow tall and thick as a windbreak for the crops, only being 'shortened' (or layered, with growing saplings half cut-through and bent down to make an impenetrable barrier) if necessary to keep livestock out. At the time of writing a hedge on the left was still in this wild state, giving a good impression of just what sort of impediment to movement such hedges were and what sort of concealment they afforded, although they didn't stop musket fire or cannon balls.

See how the ground first drops away and then rises again. This is the famous Round Hill where Skippon based his headquarters. The major part of this feature is now a private garden with lots of ornamental trees, but there is a small area of open land on the east-facing slope, which is the traditional location of Merrick's Battery. Unfortunately the well-fenced house on the summit of Round Hill renders it difficult to judge lines of sight so as to position the guns exactly. I have not tried requesting permission to roam the grounds.

Continue down the track to the third bush and turn to face north. The whole northern sector of the battlefield is laid out before you. The Enborne road is behind the hedge that crosses the middle distance. An observer here on the day would have seen the engagement between Robartes and Vavasour, and watched the Blue Auxiliaries march up into the line and Springate's troops wheel up towards the point where you are standing. In the fields beyond the Enborne road part of Middleton's cavalry manoeuvred to try to reach the flank of the Royalist line. In the far distance you should also be able to see the village of Speen and Donnington Castle,

The eastern slope of Round Hill. Skippon's third hedge is in the dip in the foreground, while Darke Lane runs along the skyline of the slope.

145

which both feature in the story of Newbury II. The two battlefields are that close.

Look across at Round Hill and its northern slope. There, towards the end of the battle, stood the Red Auxiliaries, having been brought forward to support the line and guard Merrick's exposed flank. To the right and down the hill is a small copse that marks the location of Skinner's Green, where Skippon kept his Reserve. There are only a few houses there today. As you walk back up the erstwhile lane take time to notice the nature of the fields and consider how small they must have been; then look above the trees at the water tower and think how close the royal guns actually were.

Now leave these fields and make your way back on to Essex Street. Turn right and walk west. The main road bends round to the left and passes Wash Common Farm, but there is a small road straight ahead that appears to lead to Round Hill. This is Cope Hall Lane, formerly Skinner's Green Lane, and its upper end is worth exploring on foot. This was the scene of the bloody incident related in the text, and there are several gaps in the hedge on the right through which you can see other aspects of the Round Hill fighting area. Notice Skippon's third hedge in the dip to the right. This was where the Royalist attack petered out and you can understand why, if you think of close-range musketry supported by overhead cannon-balls from the guns. Although I do have doubts about this, I am reliably informed by a re-enactor that such artillery support would have been likely.

In the hedge on the left there is another gap, next to a footpath sign and a stile. Climb over the stile and go out into the field beyond until the ground starts to fall away to the south (and indeed to the east).

STAND SIX: The Londoners' Position
This, for me, is the slope upon which the Red and Blue Regiments of the London Trained Bands made their famous stand. Driven back from their first stand, where they had been battered by the Royalist grand battery, they halted on this rising ground and took the full brunt of an attack from both Foot and Horse thrown at them by Sir Gilbert Gerard. Here the untried Londoners courageously stood their ground, performing one of the most outstanding feats of endurance in the whole of the war.

To the south-east the farm serves as a marker for their line of retreat; it also marks the direction of the Royalist attack. Behind you is Round Hill and the site of the battery. Despite the efforts of the Londoners, it was across this ground that Sir Charles Gerard's Regiment of Horse swarmed, forcing the two trained band regiments into a single ill-formed stand; some troopers even got across the lane to the right of Merrick's guns.

Go back over the stile and walk a little further down Cope Hall Lane to see Round Hill and the slope of the lane up which the Parliamentarian train had

The suggested site of the centre of the combined stand of the Red and Blue Regiments of the London Trained Bands. In the background is the house that now occupies Round Hill. The hedge in front of it was supposedly manned by musketeers from Skippon's regiments.

to haul their guns. The views beyond the hedges are not very good as there are too many trees, and the private house prevents further exploration.

It is now time to return to the car and investigate the southern sector of the field where Essex attacked and nearly broke through. Leave Battle Road and turn left into Essex Street, following the road as it bends to the left past Wash Common Farm. Continue along this road (now Enborne Street). There may or may not have been a track here in 1643, but we do know that to its right (west) were enclosures and to its left (east) was open common, scrubland with scattered bushes and trees. This was the line Essex wanted to pierce to gain access to the open high ground, for this road runs along the apex of a spine or ridge that runs south to the end of a spur before curving right towards Biggs' Hill and Holtwood. This is (or was) Wash Common. Unfortunately for battlefield historians it is now a series of housing developments, and more are spreading on to the other side of the road. Enborne Street, however, is useful for orientation, as roughly one might allocate the ground to the right as Essex's and to the left Rupert's.

As you drive along look out for Wheatlands Lane on the right; it runs westwards down the slope and under the ring road to Enborne. This is one of the major routes used by Essex's Foot to come up on to the high ground during the first advance. On the other side of the road, approximately in Blossom Field (near the houses at the top end of Conifer Crest), was where Mainwaring's Regiment was overrun and the Red and the Blue Trained Bands made their advance to plug the gap between Essex's and Skippon's wings. Somewhere on this plateau, before the ground falls away again down Normay Rise, they stood their ground at 'far less than twice musket shot' in front of the royal guns, which did their best to blow them to pieces. Once again a glance up at the water tower will help you gauge position and distance.

Some of the best views of the country over which Essex's Foot advanced can be gained from the western side of the cricket field, and it is worth asking permission to walk round and see, although during the summer months the trees obscure so much. To the west the top of the cricket club slope overlooks Lush Gully. Across the road to the east is a housing estate. on the site of the bitterest fighting for the Common. It was on this land that Rupert's Horse finally forced Stapleton's to retire, and where regiments from Belasyse's and Sir Gilbert Gerard's Tertios finally drove back Holbourne's and Barclay's Brigades as well as Essex's own regiment. I have driven around this estate several times and although it is possible to interpret the flat ground as the place where the majority of the contest for the common was waged, only the road names now recall the battle: among them you will see Meldrum, Holbourne, Merrick and Balfour. It is not a rewarding task and photo-opportunities are non-existent. However, all along the line of Enborne Street, as it runs along this spine, the Parliamentarian infantry defended a hedge during the closing stages of the battle.

To see where Stapleton's breakthrough was made, drive a little further along the road. As it begins a sweeping curve to the right you will see a farm gate on the left, where you can safely pull in and park. The modern name for this area is Mount Pleasant but it may take its name from a local farm.

STAND SEVEN: The Cavalry Battle
The roadway and the fields to the east and south-east saw the major engagements between Rupert and Stapleton. To the east there is a slight gully running up from the south and the fighting might have raged across it. It is feasible that over these fields Rupert, Caernarvon and Wilmot charged their veteran brigades and Stapleton's threw them back.

The site of the gap from which the Parliamentarians debouched on to the common has long gone but it seems reasonable to suggest the common gave way to enclosures somewhere along this curving section of road, possibly just round the bend and down the slope. According to the Rocque map, the common was on the high ground and the enclosures began where the ground began to fall away. It is a great pity that such a crucial location in the story of the battle is not easily definable, although with imagination the fields can still swirl with Horse and the hedges swarm with dragoons!

Walking and understanding this area is not easy, although a public foot-path threads its way down Trundle Hill. Woods have grown up, farms have been built all over the area, and on the main plateau more housing has gone up around Enborne Lodge and a reservoir has been excavated. Added to this, traffic in the area travels too fast for anybody's safety. Take great care and seek permission if you want to go on to private land. Numerous signs make it clear that people are not welcome, even if they are battlefield enthusiasts.

Return to the car. Drive down the hill and turn left down Andover Drove. Just before the junction there is another convenient pull-in in which to park, giving a fine view of the rising ground to the east up which the Horse on Stapleton's extreme right is said to have advanced. This is unproven and unlikely, but you should now be able to appreciate the gradient of the slope. Ignore the cross road, for even as late as 1761 it appears there was no lane along the bottom of the En Valley.

Turn around and drive back up to Enborne Street, turning left at the T-junction. Carry on down the slope, round the bend and over the A34. It is well worth stopping on the bridge and looking back eastwards, for this is the route of Stapleton's Horse up to the common, and over to the left are the fields which a lot of Essex's Foot must have crossed.

Drive on, passing Boames Lane on your right, until you come to a sign-post for Ball Hill on the left. Stop near here. The house to the west of this junction is Biggs' Cottage, where tradition says Essex made his headquarters and spent the night before the battle. This may just be Money, and Essex's headquarters was nearer his baggage. Turn around and go left up Boames Lane. Near the crest seek a safe parking spot to have a look at the high ground to the east across the dual carriageway.

STAND EIGHT: The Decision to Fight

This summit might have been one of the places from where Essex and his staff made their evening reconnaissance. Although there are far more trees today, the lie of the land is obvious. If local intelligence said there was a common up there with access to the Aldermaston, Reading and hence London roads, and scouts reported those heights to be virtually unmanned, then the solution to Essex's strategic dilemma becomes easy to understand. The tactical decisions must have come later, when Round Hill was reported as being unoccupied.

Continue along Boames Lane, following it down the other side of the hill. The fields here were Crockham Heath, where Essex's army camped before the battle. Turn right, keeping Long Copse on your left. As the trees clear there is a field to the north which is supposed to be where Mainwaring's Regiment finally halted and rallied after being cut up on the common. Follow the road as it goes under the A34 and take the first turning to the left (keeping straight on will take you up Wheatlands Lane to Enborne Street). This winding road, known today as Skinner's Green Lane, is sometimes used as a rat-run at peak traffic times, so be careful. It takes you along the rear of Skippon's position, past the bottom of the west side of Round Hill, where Cope Hall Lane joins from the right. In the seventeenth century there was a hamlet known as Skinner's Green at this junction and an expanse of common cattle pasture, The Green itself, about 100m to the north-west. Regrettably there is not much to see today, although if you carry on and park in the lay-by at the next sharp left-hand bend you will get a good view of the whole area.

The fields of Skinner's Green, where Skippon posted his ever-decreasing Reserve. Round Hill is to the right and the water-tower to the east can just be seen.

STAND NINE: Skinner's Green

Here and on either side of the lane further north waited Skippon's Reserve, gradually decreasing in size as he committed unit after unit to the battle. One can perhaps ascribe one reserve location to Skinner's Green Farm as there is a small fresh stream and a pond close by. A ready water supply was a must for waiting troops. There is not much to see here and little to exercise the imagination but it all helps to fully understand the events. Continue along the lane, running parallel to the dual carriageway, and at the T-junction turn right into Enborne Road. There are parking places on the left and right as you head towards Newbury. I recommend parking in one of the lay-bys on the right, but again be careful as big lorries use this minor road and some cars travel along it much too fast.

STAND TEN: The Enborne Road

This is the route Robartes had to block and his regiments must have been on both sides of the road. Out to the left was a collection of enclosures called Guyer's Fields, where most of Middleton's Horse sought to turn Vavasour's flank, but the ground was not drained in 1643 and was far too boggy for cavalry to move easily. We are not told if Vavasour marched out from Newbury itself or came down via the valley once the ground opposite had been secured by Byron, but he would have sought a fight somewhere along

NEWBURY II	
Campaign:	The King's Cornish Campaign
War period:	First Civil War
Outcome:	Indecisive Parliamentarian victory
County:	West Berkshire
Place:	Newbury/Speen
Terrain:	Enclosed fields, commons and built-up areas
Date:	27 October 1644
Start:	3:00pm
Duration:	2 hours
Armies:	Parliament: Earl of Manchester and Sir William Waller
	Royalist: King Charles I and Prince Maurice
Numbers:	Parliament: 12,000 Foot and 5,000 Horse
	Royalist: 5,000 Foot and 3,500 Horse
Losses:	About 500 per side
OS Explorer map:	158
Grid Reference:	46–47:67–68

this road. Perhaps he got as far as where the buildings are today and then fell back. We cannot be sure as the accounts are not detailed enough. The best guess at a position for Robartes's defensive stand, with his light guns in the roadway, would be where the double-hedged lane dropping down from the high ground in front of Round Hill joins the Enborne road. The Rocque map shows it as a crossroads, but today the northern section has been ploughed out, although it is still quite discernable as an old road. Once more agricultural development has robbed us of an important site, although by taking an 'eye line' a good approximation can be reached.

Stand Ten and the fight on the Enborne road concludes the circular tour. The Enborne road will take you directly back into central Newbury for some well-earned refreshment, or you could head west and seek out one of the many village pubs offering excellent food. If you have a taste for further exploration, following the road will take you along Essex's approach march and to Hungerford where signposts for Aldbourne direct you back to the beginning of the battle. Or you could begin to explore Newbury II . . .

The site of Newbury II has been virtually lost to development, although tracing Waller's flanking march can be an enjoyable trip. To be frank, the rest of the field requires a great deal of imagination, although a few important sites can be visited.

In the west there is still open ground in the shape of Speen Lawn north of the A4, although it was flattened and levelled by bulldozers to provide a mobile-home site for the workers on the Newbury by-pass. The dual carriageway itself cuts through the Royalist position and has destroyed the location of the barricade, although the crest of the slope upon which Maurice positioned his guns is still discernable. Speen itself underwent a lot of rebuilding during the eighteenth and nineteenth centuries and although it remains relatively picturesque, there are few buildings that would have witnessed the street fighting of 1644. In the centre the famous Speenhamland hedge and the surrounding fields have gone. On both sides of the A4 there are housing developments and finding anything that might relate to the fighting here is impossible. Shaw House is now a school but it is at least still there. There too one can see several banks, which some believe were once ancient earthworks incorporated into Lisle's outlying defences. Clay Hill too has been built over, but not before it was ravaged for its base material by the brick-making trade.

In April 1646 Boys and his garrison of Donnington Castle finally fell to a third siege by Dalbier and marched out with their weapons, colours and drums. Today the site is in the care of English Heritage and is consequently preserved for the nation, although the battering it took from the Parliamentarian artillery during the sieges is very evident. Only the foundations remain of the curtain wall and its twin-towered gatehouse has been gutted. The earthworks, however, are fascinating, despite being much worn down, and they form a good record of seventeenth-century field defences.

To find Newbury II

Follow exactly the same directions as given for Newbury I, parking the car in the same place.

A battlefield tour for the Second Battle of Newbury
STAND ONE: Maurice's Front Line
This time face north. On the hill to the north-east Donnington Castle stands out, and you should see an oak tree in the middle of a small field to the north of the A4/Stockcross roundabout. This tree became a rallying point during the protest against the Newbury by-pass, when it was occupied by protesters and even had a tent perched in its branches. It grows upon a slight bank which is believed by many battlefield interpreters to be the remains of Maurice's trenches, which cut the Great West Road and defended Speen. Tradition says it was here that the guns captured by the Royalists at Lostwithiel were recaptured and turned against them.

It is possible to walk this field and despite the desecration you can get some sense of the land upon which that tremendous struggle took place. Judging by the height of what is left, you can find the crest of this slight north–south ridge and hence Maurice's line. A particular line of research has found an alternative location for the barricade, placing it in the V created between the A4 and the road to Stockcross. Unfortunately that field was bulldozed flat to provide a level surface for the temporary on-site accommodation for the road-workers and their security guards. This whole area is key to the battle. It is a shame that the diggers displaced and piled up so much earth, altering the very landscape. If the dual carriageway could be filled in, then we could see where Maurice's men stood. Looking north along the line of the A34 it is possible to distinguish the trees bordering the Lambourne in the bottom of the dip. Between there and this rise Cromwell's cavalry pushed their way through the wet ground, trying to get out of the enclosures; if you now turn around and look south, at about the same distance away is the Kennet, and between it and where you are standing Balfour's cavalry did likewise.

Return to the car and loop round to follow the A4 into Newbury, but turn right by the war memorial, signposted for Speen church. The road narrows and older houses appear on both sides. These were (or now stand on the site of) the houses that Skippon's men had to clear in the short, sharp and bloody fight for Speen village. As you follow the road towards Newbury you will see another signpost for the church, and a turning to the right which leads down to it. If you have time it is worth a look but the current building is a very Victorian structure, although local legend says it was fought over! As you drive along Speen Lane you run into Speenhamland and the area where Skippon had to fight from hedge to hedge, although there is nothing left today. There is, however, a right turn down Hill Lane. Take it and go all the way to the bottom, where the lane widens and there is room to park.

STAND TWO: Balfour's Advance

Hill Lane leads to a Thameswater installation on the Kennet, but the lane itself also goes east and west. Walk west along the unmade roadway past a series of small fields. Before reaching a former railway bridge you should be able to see Speen church through the trees. Cross-referencing these hedges to the map in the museum and the various accounts of the battle, they are more than likely to be in the location where Balfour swept 'south of the church' and then fought his way through a series of small enclosures.

Walk back to the T-junction and continue along the track. The patchwork

Balfour's enclosures west of Hill Lane. This area gives any visitor a good idea of the small size of the enclosures and the closed nature of the ground. It is easy to see why this was not cavalry country!

of small fields continues east of Hill Lane until houses and gardens take over. However, at the eastern end of the track near a set of bollards preventing vehicle access there is another north–south lane, called 'the pedestrian bit of Northcroft Lane', beyond which is the open space of Goldwell Park. The land is flat at the bottom of the Kennet valley and slopes upwards towards the Old Bath Road. The Northcroft Leisure Centre now occupies a lot of the flat land but the whole area is quite understandable. One can never be certain, but if the lane marked the site of the southern portion of a hedge, then Bennet's Brigade was first broken in the area of the leisure centre and its car parks, and Stuart's charge came down the slope into the flank of the mêlée.

Placing that action here also makes sense as the distance to Northbrook Street is very short and the shattered brigade would not have been able to disperse before being intercepted and rallied. It is also not that far from Shaw House, facilitating the rapid switch of wings for the Lifeguard which the accounts demand.

Return to the car and drive back up Hill Lane. Turn right on to Speen Lane and continue to the junction with the Old Bath Road. If you want to judge how far Goldwell Park is from the centre of the town, turn right at the first roundabout and follow signs for the Northcroft Leisure Centre, otherwise continue across the junction and go left at the next mini-roundabout. This will lead to the A4 Waitrose roundabout, where you should follow the signs for Donnington up the B4494. Turn left into Grove Road, signposted for Bagnor and Welford, and go past a golf course on the right. Park as near as you can to the junction where a left turn leads back up to Speen and the main thoroughfare bears right and becomes Lambourne Road.

STAND THREE: Cromwell's Attack

Cromwell used the Lambourne road to bring his troops from Boxford to Speen, and it was here, to Skippon's left, that the Eastern Horse tried to force its way into the open fields. It would appear that Cromwell's men and Goring's may have fought on the golf course! This area of land does have public footpaths across it but it was totally re-landscaped in 1979, and it would seem drainage was also incorporated as the land is now reasonably firm. In 1644 the soft going here would have taken the impetus out of any charge, so manoeuvring and fighting on the upper reaches of the slope would be more feasible. To the more romantically inclined, it might be that Cleveland's Brigade hit Cromwell's men on the Donnington Grove Country Club's seventeenth fairway and drove them back beyond the ditch, but we cannot site events here with any accuracy.

Look up at Donnington Castle. The whole area would have been under its guns, confirming both Waller's and Cromwell's comments, although not

The golf course and possible site of Goring's charge across the higher (and thus drier) ground.

subscribing to their exaggeration. Some very keen explorers may wish to drive around the housing estates between Grove Road and the A4, looking for the site of the Foot battle fought there, but I find this unrewarding. Instead I recommend you return to the car, and take the left turn back to Speen, joining the A4 at the Hare and Hounds pub. Turn left. Cross the Waitrose roundabout and continue along the main road to join the large A4/A339 roundabout complex. Once under the road bridge, take the left-hand lane. At the traffic lights leave the roundabout on the B4009 signposted for Hermitage. Drive north, through old Shaw village, and cross the Kennet. Ignoring the signs to Shaw House, turn right up Kiln Road and then after 750m turn left up Stoney Lane for Cold Ash. This is Clay Hill. Waller's Way joins this road from the right as it runs up this once-commanding promontory, now sadly ravaged by the brick industry for its clay, and developed for housing. As the road reaches the summit the houses thin out and fields appear on the right. On the crest there is a pull-in on the right next to a crudely scrawled 'No Trespassing' sign. This is a convenient place to park as it's off the road, and opposite is a poorly marked public footpath along the side of a set-back bungalow called Runways. The track is overgrown but it leads to a stile and Messenger's Copse. There is a break in the trees to the left just after the stile and you emerge on to the hillside with a commanding view of Shaw through a gap in the trees.

STAND FOUR: Clay Hill

We may be somewhat too far to the right, but this is probably the best view available from Clay Hill (unless you have friends who own one of the houses). Manchester's army stood on this ridge prior to descending the slopes to the south and assaulting Shaw and Shaw House. This position overlooks Shaw and with binoculars you should be able to make out the rise on which stood the royal works that held up the attack, and perhaps Shaw House itself. The intervening fields and hedgerows are clearly discernable and so too is the Curridge bridleway.

STAND FIVE: Parliamentarian Deployment

Return to the car. Take a good look at the field spread out before you and down the slope to the south, as this was the Parliamentarian deployment area where the troops formed up before the attack. They may be fields now but in 1644 this was open scrubland and well suited to the task as it is flat,

The open land to the east of Clay Hill where Manchester deployed his brigades for the Parliamentarian attacks on Shaw.

unencumbered and well out of sight, which meant Manchester and Ludlow could organise their forces in secrecy.

Drive down the hill and at the junction with the main road turn right and head back towards Shaw. At the crossroads go right up Shaw Road, the B4009, signposted for Hermitage. This becomes Long Lane. Go a mile or so up this lane and then turn around to look at the position the Parliamentarians attacked. Turn around and go back, and turn right opposite the cemetery into Highwood Close. Park here. There is an unmarked bridleway between the houses that soon emerges into a shady, tree-lined lane running along the eastern slope of Brick-kiln Hill; this is a public thoroughfare and other public footpaths run off it, especially to the left over the brow towards Shaw Farm. It is well worth exploring this bridleway.

STAND SIX: Manchester's Northern Body
This lane probably marks one of the major obstacles crossed by Manchester's men as they came down Clay Hill, crossed its lower fields and struck at Astley's forces posted north of the Lambourne. In fact if Long Lane had been the forward post of the musketeers of the Royalist forlorn hope, then it was from this bridleway that the attackers received the first ferocious volley that took the impetus out of their rolling advance. Musket balls have been discovered in the fields between here and Long Lane, and perhaps an archaeological search among these hedges would reveal more evidence to show that this was the site of the major engagement on the Parliamentarian right.

There are additional areas to explore here, such as the fields to the west, accessible via the footpaths or between the rows of garages into the housing estate on the rise north of Love Lane, although this is not that rewarding. Return to the car and head south back to the crossroads by the Lambourne bridge, and turn right for Shaw House. Pass the house on your right and look for a free public car park opposite the church through a wooden gate. Do not park on the roadside as this lane is subject to frequent parking checks, and do not drive up the road into Trinity School as they have installed a sump-breaker! Once safely parked you can explore the area on foot, although you are strongly advised not to go on to school property – where, a sad sign of our times, unknown adults are very unwelcome.

STAND SEVEN: Astley's Left
Again development has taken a heavy toll but we can work out where things were and what happened where thanks to the accounts. Staying on the public highway, walk northwards through the car park, for it was here that the Royalist cavalry under Browne was drawn up to support the house; across the old Donnington road (now Love Lane), in a field to the left of the

Shaw church. How much of the church is original and what alterations, if any, have been made remain to be investigated.

church (probably in the Vodaphone car parks), stood the hastily summoned Lifeguards and Queen's Regiment.

Walk eastwards up Love Lane. The back of Shaw House can be seen through the trees and you soon come to its north wall, from where the defenders poured fire into the Parliamentarian troopers as they drove Browne back. On the opposite side of the road are the school playing fields, very likely the site of the several engagements that stemmed Manchester's attack. Again notices instruct you to keep out of school property. It is possible to walk up a track that leads to Shaw Farm, from where you can see not only the land where the running fight took place but also the crest to the right over which the Parliamentarians poured after clearing the bridleway, but here too there are several unwelcoming notices. There is a footpath running along the eastern perimeter of Shaw House, from where you can see the earthworks that were 'improved upon' to defend the position. The north-east corner which took the brunt of the southern body's attack is unfenced, although we do not know where the Parliamentarian forces broke through. The southern bank is currently palisaded, much as it may have been during the battle. At the time of writing the house was also 'out of bounds' as a working site, but part of the building was being turned into a community centre so access should be possible in the future. For those who wish to explore this particular site further, I suggest you write to the school's headteacher and seek permission for entry to the grounds.

STAND EIGHT: Shaw House

This is a remarkable position and one of the few surviving fought-over houses. It was certainly damaged in the fighting but its banks and trees prevented it from being bombarded. Luckily it was not fired during the action nor slighted afterwards. There is a legend that the woodwork around one of the windows still bears the mark of a musket ball that smacked into its frame, narrowly missing the King's head, although it is doubtful he ever entered the building during the fight! It is easy to imagine the place thick with acrid grey smoke and crowded with musketeers frantically reloading and queuing up to take their place at the windows. This house was a fortress and you can get some idea of the ranges involved by standing at the gate, where some Parliamentarians were shot down.

The south embankment of Shaw House, now topped with a wooden fence perhaps resembling in part the palisade said to have been erected by Lisle's men.

With your back towards the main gate of Shaw House, turn left and walk down towards the village. To the right is the site of the old rectory, which was also supposedly manned. This whole lane was lined by a hedgerow, behind which there were Royalist musketeers firing into the flanks of those soldiers trying to break into the grounds of the house. Further east along Love Lane is the rise between the house and Long Lane/Shaw Road where the royal works held up the attack, which was obliged to flow around the works in the course of the assault on the house and village. It is now all lost beneath private housing. The remains of the entrenchments seen by Money in the mid-1800s have long since disappeared and there's nothing to see.

STAND NINE: Shaw Village
The old mill mentioned in the accounts is still there, albeit much altered, and so too are the houses of Old Shaw. The village was broken into by the Parliamentarians twice, first from the east in the morning and then from the north-east in the afternoon. The area of ground south of the houses towards the A4 roundabout was supposedly also contested during the diversionary attack.

The bridge is of course a modern construction but the rows of buildings flanking the road into Newbury stand on the site of the 1644 dwellings, proving that the village must have been a formidable obstacle to assault. From the east attackers would encounter a solid row of barricaded houses and walls, while any troops forcing their way across the bridge from the north would be funnelled into a point-blank killing zone between manned and fortified houses. Working out likely enfilades from Shaw against troops heading for Shaw House is easy, especially if some took the northern parts of the village before pressing on. Having explored this area, return to the car and come back to the crossroads. Turn left up Shaw Road and then go left again along Love Lane. Pass the house and the school, cross over the A339 and a short drive will take you into Donnington. Cross the B4494 and take a small road signposted to the castle, which is up a traffic-calmed lane and has its own car park.

STAND TEN: Donnington Castle
The castle and its surrounding earthworks are in the care of English Heritage and there are several interpretation boards to read, including one in Braille.

Successive bombardments and subsequent scavenging for building materials have largely destroyed the castle. Only the gatehouse towers remain of the stronghold that Boys and Earl Rivers' Regiment first held for the King. It is, however, still a spectacular sight and it is well worth climbing to the top of the mound to see the views from its shattered walls. Its small size explains why 250 Foot and 25 Horse were able to hold it, especially when you imagine the wooden palisades, shelters and piled-up rubble walls. The earthworks need investigation and reinstatement but English Heritage's finances are limited. They have done a good job clearing the site and maintaining it. The view east is limited by the surrounding trees but you can appreciate just how the castle overlooked the Oxford road and controlled the valley across to Clay Hill and the land down to the Kennet.

To the south Newbury lies before you, while to the south-west are Round Hill, Skinners' Green and the field of Newbury I. If you stand on the earth ramparts where Boys had his guns, you should see at the foot of the hill the line of trees bordering the River Lambourne and beyond them is the open grass parkland of the golf course. This open space and the slopes behind it were the main target areas for the guns, for that is where Waller's force marched forward to attack Speen and then pushed on into Speenhamland – no wonder Cromwell was not keen to expose his experienced cavalry to danger by advancing under flanking fire from this place.

The fall of Donnington Castle is another story, but it is advisable to tour the whole site and, if you have time, to explore Castle Woods to the west to look at the works dug by the 1646 attackers. Stand Ten and Donnington Castle conclude the circular tour of Newbury II. Return to the village and turn right on to the old Oxford road (the B4494), which will take you directly back into central Newbury for some well-earned refreshment. However, if you have a taste for further exploration, turn left at the Waitrose roundabout and head east on the A4 to Thatcham, where Waller's famous night march began.

A battlefield tour of Waller's March
This is designed as a driving tour of some 20 miles through the attractive Berkshire countryside and villages. En route there are plenty of places to park and enjoy the view or even picnic, and there are ample public houses for refreshment. It is best to go in the same direction as Waller's army but remember that you are following the march of a whole army, and not everyone would have been on the road; the force would have spread out on both sides into the fields and heathland.

Begin at Stand One on the A4 bridge over the A34. Head towards Newbury on the A4, and go across the roundabout junction with the B4494. The road then comes to a complicated roundabout that passes under the A339. Follow signs for A4/Thatcham. Although Waller's headquarters were in Thatcham there is nothing relevant to see there. About 2km east of Newbury there is a conventional roundabout near a garden centre. Turn off the A4 here (before Thatcham) and head north. The road bends first right and then left in long curves. At the fork in the road go left, heading for Cold

Ash. Waller's force came together from quarters all over this area, including the hamlets of Henwick, Ashmore Green and Bucklebury, which can all be visited by taking minor roads.

However, the main route runs north-west up Hermitage Road, then across the bottom of Slanting Hill and through the eastern end of modern Curridge, where it joins the B4009. Turn right and head for Hermitage. Just beyond Faircross Plantation on the left there is a crossroads signposted left to Chievely; this may not be the original road as Doctor's Lane further north is more probable, but it is the main road and not too serious a shortcut. You soon rejoin the old road as it heads west, crossing the M4 and passing Priors Court, which is now a school. Somewhere along this hook north and west the small cavalry force from Sir John Boys' Donnington garrison tried their limited attack, but as yet we do not know exactly where.

Cross the bridge over the A34 and enter the southern end of Chievely. Pass the Red Lion public house and then take the rather sudden left turn into School Road, signposted for Winterbourne and Boxford. The road soon heads directly west again but as it climbs North Heath it turns sharp left. Waller's men would have gone directly forward up the grassy lane on to the

Boxford bridge and mill. Waller's vanguard attacked over the bridge, driving back the Royalists guarding the crossing.

higher heath where they rested. There is still a large farm in the area but its tracks are private and not accessible. Continue on the road south to a junction with the Wantage road (the B4494). If you wish to take a closer look at the heath turn right here and go up the slope; on the crest is the well-known fish restaurant, The Crab at Chievely. Ironically it was along this road that Waller's troopers intercepted the provision wagons and shared out their contents.

If you do not want to see the heath, or, having seen it, wish to continue the tour, head towards Newbury and go under the M4, but almost immediately turn right for Winterbourne. Drive through the village, passing the Winterbourne Arms, and at its southern end turn right for Boxford. Do not carry on southwards as this road leads to Bagnor, which was in Royalist hands and fortified. The countryside is more rolling here, with short climbs and descents until it finally drops into Boxford, where a left turn will bring you to the bridge across the Lambourne river.

Parking is easy and the water-meadows are worth a look, although little has been discovered about the scattering of Douglas's grand guard posted here. Return to your car. Cross the river and dog-leg left and right to the junction with the Lambourne Low Road. The Bell will be on your right. For Cromwell's route to Speen turn left, and follow this road towards Newbury, passing through Hunt's Green and Woodspeen. For Balfour's and Skippon's route cross over this road and climb the hill, signposted to Hoe Benham. Once on the plateau there is another crossroads. Turn left on to the B4000 and proceed towards Newbury, passing through Stockcross and past the Vine Hotel to the A4/B4000 roundabout and the adjacent bridge over the A34. You are now back at Stand One.

Chapter Nine

HELPFUL INFORMATION

When visiting battlefields it is always nice to know where you can find things and amenities that make the day out easy to manage. This includes everything from public toilets to supermarkets, and from cosy pubs to modern libraries. The two battlefields in this book are situated a short drive away from the busy Thames Valley town of Newbury and thus one can assume a wealth of choice in the town centre. Rather than try to list everything you can do or see, I have chosen several highlights to single out for mention. I also award battlefield walkers' star (*) ratings on a scale of 1 (poor) to 5 (excellent). Obviously the selection of recommendations and ratings will reflect my tastes and opinions but they might help make your visit more enjoyable. The following information was correct in 2007.

Where to Find Information

The Battlefields
Regrettably there is no battlefield interpretation at the site of either conflict and the only monument is that to Viscount Falkland, killed at Newbury I, which lies on the Andover Road (the A343) near the Gun Inn on the eastern edge of that battlefield. On-site tour help is non-existent, there are no way markers and battlefield walkers will need to be aware of modern road names to find their way around. Rating: *

Tourist Information Office
The central office is in Wharf Street, off the Market Place, at the end of an Elizabethan-looking row of gable-balconied buildings; in fact the Corn Hall and a granary were linked sympathetically fairly recently. This is a typical tourist-oriented town service. Although it boasts a good array of local information and the staff are welcoming and friendly, their battlefield knowledge is understandably limited and the information given them about the area's

two major battles is woefully inadequate. If you want information about what's happening in Southampton or Bristol you will find it here in plenty, but there is precious little about Newbury's military past. There is one pamphlet with a simple map but it says little and is rather uninteresting. Use this place to enhance your stay in the town or area but don't count on it for battlefield-related stuff. Rating: Generally ****; Battlefield *

Museum
The museum is situated in the same row of buildings as the Tourist Information Office but at the Corn Hall end nearer the Market Place. Entrance is free and the staff are both welcoming and very willing to help, although they too are poorly supplied with battle information. You can at least buy several battle-related books here, notably Keith Roberts' excellent *The First Battle of Newbury, 1643* (Oxford: Osprey, 2003), and a Heritage Guide pamphlet entitled 'The Civil War in Newbury'. I was fortunate also to acquire a photocopy of Rocque's map although it was not on general display or sale. Upstairs in the museum itself there is a small display of artefacts pertaining to the battles, notably a selection of weapons, armour and ammunition collected from both sites, as well as a china bowl from a house in East Woodhay which is said to have been used by Cromwell during the post-Newbury II operations. However, there is no explanation of events except for a route map for Waller's march from Shaw to Speen. There is good waxwork-type dummy of a Parliamentarian trooper, and I am told the whole display is due for a major renovation soon. Rating ***

Library
Continue eastwards down Wharf Street a short way then cross the road and there, in the middle of its own car park, is the town's modern library. It is in a fine modern but traditionally designed building, and you will find there a collection that attempts to cover everything written about the battle – secondary sources, that is. The local collection is interesting, with a selection of maps and books, including the works of Walter Money, the doyen of Newbury's local history. His work should now be taken with a good pinch of salt, as his Royalist bias is far worse than my own Parliamentarian leaning. The staff are very helpful and nothing seems too much for them. If you have the time, an hour or so browsing here can be rewarding. Rating ***

Book Shops
The town has several chain bookstores but the real gem in Newbury is the Invicta Bookshop in Cromwell Place. This is a real old-fashioned second-hand book emporium which boasts an unusually rich stock of military books and pamphlets. Although it is just off the main shopping street, it is

not easy to find. Start on the west side of Northbrook Street, north of the river, and turn left down the alley opposite Marks & Spencer's. It looks unpromising, but there is a beauty salon and some offices on the left and a few metres beyond is a converted terraced cottage with the Invicta sign. The military history section is 'in the back room' on the west wall – happy hunting! Rating *****

Other Things to Do and See

Newbury is a small friendly town with a good selection of shops, and a bustling market on Thursdays and Saturdays. Newbury racecourse is only a short distance from both the town and Wash Common, and a combined battlefield and horseracing weekend might suit some people. For those who enjoy walking and want to see more of the countryside than just the fields of conflict, the Berkshire Downs offer some breathtaking and beautiful

The Falkland Memorial on the Andover Road.

countryside, not to mention the tranquil old pathways beside the Kennet and Avon Canal.

The one edifice you can visit is the Falkland Memorial on Wash Common, at the junction of the A343 Andover road and Monkey Lane/Essex Street. Like so many of our battlefield markers it is Victorian, having been erected in 1878 through the efforts of historian Walter Money; his brother James was the designer. A lot of the finance came from a descendant of the Earl of Caernarvon, whose estate is at nearby Highclere Castle, and there is a tale that although the monument was intended to commemorate the dead of both sides, the Earl insisted that the dedication on one side be only to the Royalist dead, and had his own family cipher added too! The other inscriptions are in Latin from Livy, Greek from Thucydides and English from Burke.

The Gun Inn opposite is said to have been there during the battle and was used briefly by the King, but if there was a hostelry of some description on the site at the time, it must have been totally rebuilt. There is another local story that the inn was built on the site of another gun battery that fired in conjunction with the one on the other side of the road. Unfortunately, placing a battery there would have proved hazardous to Byron's men and a lack of hard evidence makes this unlikely.

Falkland's name is also linked to a building known as Falkland Garth, a period farmhouse where his body was supposedly taken immediately after he was killed. Today the farm has gone and the house is enclosed by more modern housing.

Although there is nothing specific to see in the town itself, you might care to take a walk in Victoria Park, north of the Kennet and inside the ring road. This was the location of the Royalist baggage train, and although it extended across the car park to the high street one can appreciate how its distant location from the battlefield would not have helped ammunition supply or succouring the wounded. The site of the main Royalist camp is now lost beneath housing south of the river. It purportedly extended southward from the area of the railway station up the side of the slope towards Wash Common on either side of the A343. The only open ground to be found in this area today are the fields of St Bartholomew's School, although even this has been dramatically changed to accommodate generations of schoolboy sportsmen.

Another of Newbury's claims to fame is its role in the development of the canal system in the 1700s, and the British Waterways Visitor Centre is always a source of intriguing fascination. Wyld Court Gardens too will provide any visitor with a good day out and plenty to discover and admire.

Newbury has two theatres, the Corn Exchange Theatre in the centre of town and the Watermill Theatre at Donnington. Both stage a variety of performances and between them cater for a wide range of tastes. However, they are sometimes closed, so it is worth calling at the Information Centre to find out what's on.

Not everyone likes to spend whole days on battlefields, and if you are touring with a group or a family then other interests must also be catered for. So while the walker is out touring the site, or when the enthusiast has had enough, here are some perhaps useful tips. Newbury has the usual choice of mainstream chain stores and is suffering the 'sameness blight' as many of our towns. Northbrook Street, north of the River Kennet, has Woolworth's, Tesco/Metro and Marks & Spencer's, as well as the fiercely independent Camp Hodson – last seen with a *tableau-vivant* of a semi-naked man in the window! South of the river in Bartholomew Street is the Kennet Centre, a shopping mall with Debenham's and TKMaxx plus a number of specialist shops, including those trading in country clothes and accoutrements. No visit to Newbury can be called complete without a visit to Griffin's butcher's shop, a carnivores' paradise on the bridge over the Kennet in the centre of town; it is quite unmissable, usually due to the queues waiting to be served. Griffin's specialises in cooked meats and pies, and offers all sorts of other delicacies. I recommend their pork and apple pie for a picnic, or a family steak and kidney pie to take home, or why not try an individual raised pork pie to eat on the battlefield. Rating *****

Toy and model shops can also be found, but apart from the ubiquitous Games Workshop the military modeller or wargamer is poorly served. Rating *

Where to Stay

Although there are several luxury hotels in the vicinity, especially northwest of the town, there is not a wide selection of hotels in central Newbury. The Tourist Information Office issues an annual glossy brochure called 'Welcome to Berkshire', which lists places to stay and eat. The Hilton is conveniently placed for Newbury I, being on the west side of Wash Common in the southern sector of Newbury Retail Park. It is a standard Hilton with the usual Hilton prices. Rating ***

In town the most obvious choice is the Queen's Hotel in the Market Place. Accommodation prices currently start around £50 and they do have a large family room. There is a good selection of food available, including tapas, at lunchtime and a delightful covered courtyard bar with Eldridge Pope on hand-pump. It also has its own car park and restaurant. You can take a look and make a reservation via www.roomattheinn.info Rating ****

Newbury has a small number of bed and breakfast homes, and details are available from the Tourist Office.

Where to Find Refreshments

On Newbury I there are two pubs on the Falkland roundabout in the north-west corner of Wash Common. The landlord and staff of the Gun Inn are friendly and welcoming, but know little about the battle, but they do stock an array of cask ales and serve an extensive range of good food plus snacks. Across the road is the Old Bell. On the Enborne road on the outskirts of Hamstead Marshall is a Wadsworth's pub called the Craven Arms, while the White Hart in the village itself is renowned for its restaurant. On the southern flank there is an Arkell's pub, the Woodpecker, while on the high land off Enborne Street in the grounds of the cricket club is the Bowler's Arms.

On Newbury II all the surrounding villages have their pub, most of which do reasonable food and real ale; some even offer accommodation. Shaw has the Cock Inn (Greene King), Donnington the Three Horseshoes (Ushers) and Speen the Hare and Hounds, which is also a hotel. I have not visited them all so am reluctant to recommend any particular establishment.

The town of Newbury abounds in public houses and cafés, and the variety seems endless. You can choose from the traditional to the trendy, from the up-market to the cheap and cheerful. Some pubs are family oriented while some are typical locals that do not welcome children; one or two do not welcome strangers. Most pubs serve food or snacks and there are cafés tucked away throughout the town, and although I bewail the loss of 'greasy-spoons', you can still get good service, tasty food and value for money. You can also find assorted junk-food palaces and coffee-shops.

The Gallery Coffee Shop between the Tourist Information Office and the museum is a good place to sit and relax after a study session. It is welcoming, offers decent coffee and provides a wide range of sweet and savoury snacks, including cream teas; it also provides a take-away service for that battlefield picnic. Rating ***

Weavers' Coffee Shop can be found in Weavers' Walk, off the west side of Northbrook Street. It offers excellent toasted sandwiches and good cappuccino served outside in good weather; it does not have much of a view and is not a fashionable venue 'to be seen at', but it is a nice place to sit and relax. Rating ****

Scoffers, near the top of Northbrook Street, is a sandwich café. It boasts that it serves the best coffee in town but its tea isn't bad either, and its sandwiches are well-filled and not as expensive as elsewhere. It has a minimalist setting but the staff are efficient and very friendly. Rating ***

South of the river Caramelle is a coffee shop-cum-delicatessen opposite the Kennet Centre. Rating ***

Evening restaurants centre on the erstwhile Royalist headquarters of

Cheap Street, south of the Market Place. There is nothing much left of seventeenth-century Newbury to see there, but within a 50m radius are the Laurel, Nawab and Prezzo for Chinese, Indian and Italian food respectively, while the Empire offers traditional British food and The Plaice is a fish'n'chip shop. Opposite is the King Charles Tavern, a Greene King pub with interesting multi-national food and a range of fizzy beers. My top restaurant in town is The Square in Weavers' Walk. They have breakfast, morning snack, lunch and dinner menus, and although they concentrate on fine dining, they cater for all tastes and most pockets, with children under 12 at half-price. It is a pleasant venue using good fresh ingredients and offering simple, elegant cooking. Rating *****

Other Amenities

The railway station south of the Kennet Centre is easy to find and is obviously handy for getting into Newbury itself. Services are frequent and connections with London are good. However, as both fields are on the outskirts and on opposite sides of town transport to and from as well as around them will be a problem unless you can fund a hire car or have a taxi all day!

Public toilets are not plentiful. There is a reasonably large and clean public convenience in the south-east corner of the Kennet Centre, otherwise I would advise making use of those found in pubs and cafés or larger stores.

Newbury is full of car parks. You can choose any style, ranging from patrolled, covered bays to on-street parking just outside the constricted centre. You can find limited-stay free parking in certain streets, and if you object to paying parking fees to take your business to a town's traders then you can park outside the charging zone if you don't mind a short walk. The Kennet Centre has a large covered car park with lifts to the shops, and Sainsbury's on the eastern ring road allows a couple of hours' parking free and then charges, but will redeem the ticket cost on in-store purchases. One of my favourite places to park is opposite the Tourist Office as it is central and not too expensive. In general, parking charges vary according to the 'service' provided. There are usually spaces available almost everywhere, unless you decide to go on a Saturday morning, but even then there is always a frequent turnover.

FURTHER READING

As this is not an academic work I have chosen to produce a selected bibliography, with entries chosen from the more accessible sources, to enable readers to delve further into the fascinating stories of the two battles of Newbury.

Primary Printed Sources

Anon, *A True Relation of the Late Expedition of His Excellency Robert Earle of Essex for the Relief of Gloucester* (London, 1643).

Ashe, S., *A True Relation of the the Most Chiefe Occurences, as at and since the late Battell at Newbery Late*.

British Library, *Thomason Tracts*: E108 (23): *The Parliament's Resolution concerning the Volunteers that are to be raised under the Earl of Essex* (1642).

Bulstrode, Sir Richard, *Memoirs and Reflections* (originally published London, 1721) in C.H. Firth (ed.), *English Historical Review* (Oxford, 1895), vol. X.

Clarendon, Edward Hyde, Earl of, *The History of the Rebellion and Civil Wars in England* (Oxford, 1843).

Digby, Lord (attributed), *A True and Impartial Relation of the Bataille betwixt His Majestie's Army and that of the Rebels Neare Newbury in Berkshire* (Oxford, 1643).

Eldred, W., *The Gunners' Glasse* (London, 1646).

Firth, C.H. (ed.), *The Memoirs of Edmund Ludlow*, 2 vols (1894).

Foster, H., *A True and Exact Relation of the Marchings of the Two Regiments of the Trained Bands of the City of London* (London, 1643).

Philip, I.G., *Journal of Sir Samuel Luke*, 2 vols (Oxford: Oxfordshire Record Society, 1947).

Roy, I. (ed.), *The Papers of Captain Henry Stevens, Waggon-Master-General to King Charles I* (Oxford: Oxfordshire Record Society, 1962).

Roy, I. (ed.), *The Royalist Ordnance Papers, 1642–6* (Oxford: Oxfordshire Record Society, 1963–4).

Symonds. R., *Diary of the Marches of the Royal Army* (1644).
Walker, Sir E., *Historical Discourses upon Severall Occasions* (1705).
Ward, R., *Animadversions of Warre* (London, 1639)

Secondary Printed Sources

Barratt, J., *Cavaliers. The Royalist Army at War 1642–1646* (Stroud: Sutton, 2000).

Barratt, J., *The First Battle of Newbury* (Stroud: Tempus, 2005).

Blackmore, D., *Arms and Armour of the English Civil Wars* (London: Royal Armouries, 1990).

Burne, A. and Young, P., *The Great Civil War* (London: Eyre & Spottiswood, 1959).

Didsbury, D., *Berkshire in the Civil War* (manuscript, 1978).

Featherstone, D., *The Battlefield Walker's Handbook* (Airlife, 1998).

Firth, C.H., *'Journal of Rupert's Marches'*, English Historical Review (1898, vol. XIII), 729–41.

Firth, C.H., *Cromwell's Army* (London: Methuen, 1902).

Gardiner, R.S., *The Great Civil War*, 4 vols (London: Longmans, republished 1987).

Gruber von Arni, E.E., *Justice to the Maimed Soldier* (Aldershot: Ashgate, 2001).

Hall, A.R., *Ballistics of the Seventeenth Century* (Cambridge University Press, 1952).

Holmes, C., *The Eastern Association in the English Civil War* (1974).

Money, W., *The First and Second Battles of Newbury* (London, 1881).

Moon, J., *A Brief Relation of the Life and Memoirs of John, Lord Balasyse*, H.M.C. Ormonde Mss (London, 1903).

Newman, P., *Biographical Dictionary of Royalist Officers 1642–1660* (New Jersey, 1981).

Paddock, J., 'The Storming of Cirencester', manuscript (Cirencester, Cotswold Museum Services, 2006)

Peachey, S. and Turton, A., *Old Robin's Foot* (Leigh on Sea: Partizan Press, 1987).

Peacock, E., *The Army Lists of the Roundheads and Cavaliers* (London: Chatto & Windus, 1874).

Reid S., *Officers and Regiments of the Royalist Army* (Leigh on Sea: Partizan Press, 1992).

Reid, S., *All the King's Armies, A Military History of the Civil Wars 1642–1651* (Spellmount, 1998).

Roberts, K., *The First Battle of Newbury, 1643* (Oxford: Osprey, 2003).

Rodgers, H.C.B., *Battles and Generals of the Civil Wars* (London: Seeley Service, 1968).

Roy, I., *The Royalist Ordnance Papers, 1642–6*, 2 vols (Oxfordshire Record Society, 1964).

Scott, C., Turton, A. and Gruber von Arni, E.E., *Edgehill, the Battle Reinterpreted* (Barnsley: Pen & Sword, 2004).

Spring, L., *Officers and Regiments of Waller's Army*, 2 vols (Leigh on Sea: Partizan Press, 1989).

Turton, A., *The Chief Strength of the Army, Essex's Horse 1642–1645* (Leigh on Sea: Partizan Press, 1992).

Wanklyn, M., *Decisive Battles of the English Civil War* (Barnsley: Pen & Sword, 2005).

Young, P. and Holmes, R., *The English Civil War* (London: Eyre Methuen, 1974).

Young, P. and Tucker. N. (eds), *Military Memoirs of Captain John Gwyn* (London: Longman, 1967).

Index

This index concentrates upon general and senior officers, their armies and brigades, essential locations of action and major themes, other than when mentioned in the detail of lists. Regimental names occur so frequently in the narrative and orders of battle that indexing them is impractical.

175

Urrey, Colonel, 28

Vavasour, Sir William, 6, 37, 52, 53, 54,
    63, 116, 118, 137, 139, 140, 145, 151
Vieuville, 29

Waller, Sir William, 3, 7, 9, 69, 72, 75,
    78, 79, 80, 83, 84, 85, 86, 87, 90, 92,
93, 97, 110, 113, 121, 131, 132, 162,
    163, 164
Wantage, 27, 30
Wash Common, 32, 33, 36, 40, 41, 64, 72,
    111
Wentworth, Thomas Lord, 95, 125
Wilmot, Henry, Lord, 38, 55, 57, 119,
    148